More POACHERS CAUGHT!

Further Adventures of a Northwoods Game Warden

TOM CHAPIN

Illustrations by HAL RIME

Beaver's Pond Press, Inc.
Edina, Minnesota

Cover design and illustrations by Hal Rime
Proofreading/Editing by Steve Koskovich and Carol Frink

ISBN-13: 978-1-59298-116-8
ISBN-10: 1-59298-116-X

Library of Congress Catalog Number: 2005905834

Printed in the United States of America

First Printing: July 2005

09 08 07 06 05   5 4 3 2 1

Beaver's Pond Press, Inc.

7104 Ohms Lane, Suite 216
Edina, MN 55439
(952) 829-8818
www.BeaversPondPress.com

To order, visit *www.BookHouseFulfillment.com*
or call 1-800-901-3480. Reseller discounts available.

Adventure Publications
820 Cleveland St S
Cambridge, MN 55008

To Mary

STEWARDSHIP

Your Creator has filled the earth with all things to sustain you,

And has found them to be good. While you dwell

Among the mortals, you may partake thereof. Use

Them wisely and judiciously. Guard them

Closely, squander them not. If you are

Untrue to this sacred trust Mankind

Shall not be perpetuated but shall

Banish itself from the earth.

—Richard J. Dorer

Table of Contents

	Acknowledgments	ix
	Introduction	1
ONE	The Snow Mole	7
TWO	The Shining Fields	14
THREE	The Open Door Policy	22
FOUR	The Eager Beavers	28
FIVE	The Gross Overlimiters	34
SIX	The Hidden Threat	43
SEVEN	The Serendipitous Live-Well	52
EIGHT	The Swan Song	56
NINE	The Search for Trout	65
TEN	The Fearless Lady	73
ELEVEN	The Kitchen Capers	80
TWELVE	The Creepy Ambush	88
THIRTEEN	The Chevy Chase	94
FOURTEEN	The Faulty Success	99
FIFTEEN	The Lesson Not Learned	104
SIXTEEN	The Bear Facts	108
SEVENTEEN	The Shady Deal	113

EIGHTEEN	*The Beep-Beep Blunder*	*119*
NINETEEN	*The Perch Pursuit*	*122*
TWENTY	*The Porch Light Poachers*	*129*
TWENTY ONE	*The Fishy Tales*	*135*
TWENTY TWO	*The Webbed Tales*	*146*
TWENTY THREE	*The Case for Melvin*	*157*
TWENTY FOUR	*The Deer Camp*	*162*
TWENTY FIVE	*The Dam Sneakers*	*169*
TWENTY SIX	*The Hijacking*	*177*
TWENTY SEVEN	*The Dam Walleyes*	*183*
TWENTY EIGHT	*The Curtailed Pike*	*190*
TWENTY NINE	*The Moosecapades*	*197*
THIRTY	*The Roundabout Approaches*	*204*

Acknowledgments

This book could not have been written without the continued support and collaboration of my friends and family members who continue to encourage me on this amazing journey. At the top of this list is my wife of 36 years, Sandy, who has eagerly provided the confidence and guidance I desperately needed to complete this project. Her cheerful countenance during the many miles and long hours and her constructive feedback along the way sustained me during the arduous process of self-publishing. To her I am indebted. My three daughters, Colleen, Anita and Beth not only supported me throughout the process but helped in distribution. Longtime friends Hal and Winnie Rime are also a huge component of this endeavor. Hal's artistic talents notwithstanding, these two have continued to believe in me, and I am most grateful for that. Without the quality editing skills of brother-in-law Steve Koskovich, I would have been less able to achieve my desired results. Let me also mention my father, Gaylord, who at 88, continues to be vibrant and enthusiastic about my work.

I also acknowledge two people who died before their time in the last year, Dan Retka and Craig Backer. Dan was a Minnesota DNR Division of Waters Regional Supervisor whom I had known since 1974 and who played a part in many of my encounters. Craig, whom I had known since 1972, was a Minnesota DNR Division of Enforcement Regional Supervisor, a fellow field officer, and the best supervisor I could have had for the last eight years of my career. I valued their friendship and miss them both very much.

Introduction

The impetus to write a second book about poaching came from the positive response that the first book, *Poachers Caught!*, has generated from the reading community. I could never have anticipated the number of extraordinary and special people whom I have met while traveling through the small towns of the Midwest during a life-altering year-and-a-half journey. From the Warren Sportsmen's Club in far northwestern Minnesota, to the Duluth "Friendly" Kiwanis Club, to the Fargo, North Dakota Rotary Clubs, to the little community of Hoka in the hill country of southeastern Minnesota, everyone I encountered was incredibly personable and supportive. The 200-plus talks I have presented about the problems of poaching have provided me with the opportunity to become more informed about the tremendous public concern and appreciation for our natural resources. And it's not just the hunting and fishing population. I found very few individuals who didn't feel they have a stake in our wild areas and the creatures that inhabit them. Most nonconsumptive users (bird-watchers, hikers, campers) and motorized-recreation folks (snowmobilers, ATVers, boaters) seem to have a positive vision for the future of our natural world. They also understand that the act of poaching is a theft, a slap in the face to everyone who attempts to follow the rules.

I have also been enlightened about poaching in times past and the levels of current poaching activities. As I signed books and visited with people, many felt relaxed enough to share personal stories of poaching transgressions—usually perpetrated by their relatives. "You ARE retired?" they would first inquire. After hearing the customary "of course," each person would eagerly reminisce about poaching he or she had witnessed two to four generations ago, especially during and the decades following the Great Depression. A few examples: A middle-age woman told about accompanying her dad many times while he illegally speared walleyes in a fish shelter. "Remember to talk loudly and make lots of noise if the warden shows up," she was instructed. Apparently the illegal fish were hidden in the walls of the house and would continue to flop and bang for a time after they were speared. An elderly lady remembered when she was 8 to 10 years old her parents said that she would have to finish her homework before she could go out poaching. She was also forced to wear a headlamp, and she remembered always being cold and bloody. Another woman told me that she had 11 siblings in her family and poaching for food was a normal part of her home life while growing up. This is how her parents supplied such a large family. They always knew the local game warden was making his rounds because of the party phone line. "The warden should be there in 15 minutes," the call would come in. The family would then get together and remove the packages of illegal venison from the freezer and run it up the steep stairs to the attic. One time they placed the meat behind the barn and upon return discovered that the pigs had eaten it all.

Two lively sisters in their late '80s pretty much took over my talk at an Iron Range library. During my presentation, and in a broken Finnish accent, they revealed how they poached fish in their early years. "If you tickled the big walleyes under their bellies before grabbing them, they would stiffen up and it would be easier to get them in the gunny sack," one of them instructed. This I didn't know!

An older, grizzled gentleman at a craft show glanced at my *"Poachers Caught!"* sign and immediately looked away. "Know anything about this subject?" I inquired.

"Yes, I do," he shot back. As I enticed him to open up about his poaching history, he told me some amazing things. "I still poach," he declared in a calm manner. "You know," he said, "now that I think of it, I've never purchased a hunting or fishing license my whole life. I've shot a lot of deer over my lifetime, but I've never shot one during season!"

I thought this quite unusual during these times. His statements certainly demonstrate that "hard poaching" is still alive and well in some rural areas. I only bring these stories to light in order to illustrate that poaching is a behavior handed down from generation to generation. Every game warden knows that big-time poaching is a family tradition. Many officers have worked long enough in their careers to have arrested the younger members of the third generation of poachers.

The stories you are about to read and the experiences I shared in my first book reveal this hypothesis as a common thread in wildlife enforcement. So how do you fix it? The only way to eliminate this type of learned behavior is education. Fines and loss of equipment are not the most effective way to turn these types around. Getting in these peoples' heads with the reasons why poaching is unacceptable seems to be the best method to encourage compliance. Many poachers have turned the corner when confronted with the fact that they are indeed, thieves! Of course, there are always going to be small numbers of hunters and fishermen who will occasionally take advantage of a situation: "The ducks are flying like never before!" "The fish are biting extremely well!" "I'm going to make up for the limit I didn't get yesterday!" This is still poaching, but it stems from a different rationale. The law, however, doesn't differentiate.

I've been asked many times, "Has poaching diminished over the years?" My answer is: Yes it has . . . in certain areas. Deer and small game poaching just isn't as socially acceptable as it once was. The rural poachers have fewer areas to do their thing. More people are setting up residences where wildlife make their homes, and many neighbors don't know each other anymore. Who can they now trust to keep quiet? Fish poaching is a different matter, however. Working officers with whom I have discussed this topic all share pretty much the same thought—fish poaching is holding its own! The jury is still out on why, but I'm sure it's connected to the contemporary fisherman's investment in equipment, technology and to the lack of enforcement. There just aren't enough officers to do the job, and this situation probably exists in every state and province. It's a good thing that fewer than 5 percent of the citizens poach. This number is just an estimate, but we also speculate that less than 1 percent are caught.

I have also included in this book four stories from three fellow conservation officers and a wildlife biologist with whom I have worked. I feel the public needs to know that my stories aren't unique; all game wardens and wildlife personnel accumulate experiences that could hold an audience for days. One of the prime reasons is the fact that a game warden's job is to seek out and observe game and fish violations. Many interesting and memorable things can happen when the officer is the witness in 95 percent of violations. Dealing with folks who are caught redhanded sets the stage for all kinds of bizarre and creative behavior. And this is what I write about. Finally, to reiterate, my goal with this book is education through the use of humor and poignant reflection. The more the public can learn about the efforts and struggles expended in securing compliance with our game and fish regulations, the greater the appreciation they will have for the 6,000 game protectors nationwide who dedicate their lives to this awesome responsibility. I share these facts to the best of my recollection.

A PORTION OF ITASCA COUNTY
AND SURROUNDING AREA

ONE
The Snow Mole

I ce fishing enforcement was always one of my favorite winter
duties in Itasca County. In northern Minnesota, it's as much
a tradition to get out on the first ice of the year as it is to
participate in any deer or duck opener. On December 1, the
normal start of the northern pike spearing season, the lakes
become dotted with fish shelters, all-terrain vehicles, snowmobiles and even pickup trucks when the ice thickens to more than
a foot. It's not uncommon to have 40 inches of ice in March by
the end of a cold winter. The equipment used to fish has altered
over the years from a simple home-constructed shanty to blunt
the 30-below elements to top-of-the-line manufactured portable
cloth shelters and full-size trailer houses towed by 4X4 pickup
trucks and SUVs.

Obviously, it has become much easier for winter fishermen
to shield themselves from the weather, thereby allowing more
folks to partake in this great outdoor sport. Now throw in the
cutting edge technology of electronic fish locators, underwater
cameras and laser ice augers, and you wonder what kind of
impact these advances may have on the resource. What the
future holds and what legal limitations may be instituted down

the line is anybody's guess. I do know that most of the folks that participate in ice fishing are law-abiding and try to follow the regulations that are after all put in place to provide an equal playing field.

Of course, there will always be some characters out there on the ice who will take advantage of the legal fisherman by skirting the rules that are meant to restrict the taking and to provide a certain degree of fair chase. Two particular incidents involving violators such as these emerge as I think about the many ice fishing contacts I've experienced over the years in the county of 1000 lakes.

During an undercover fishing operation with a fellow officer on a large trout lake north of Grand Rapids, we observed an individual arriving at a fish shelter set up 400 yards from our fishing holes. Standing out on the snow-covered surface, we could scan the entire lake to observe other fishing activity. This person didn't give us a particular reason to be suspicious any more than the other half dozen people in their shelters set up around us. Within 15 minutes my partner caught a 4-pound lake trout, flopped it on the ice and quickly detected spear marks scarring the tail area.

Spearing fish through a dark house (a fish shelter where all the incoming light is shut out in order to see down into the lake under the ice) is restricted to the taking of only one type of game fish— the northern pike. Lake trout have always been off limits to this method of taking. Obviously, someone had either made a mistake or was intentionally spearing this most sought-after species.

I decided to take a walk and try to identify the names on some of the fish shelters near us. Legally, the owner's name must be clearly marked on the outside, so I took my binoculars and made an attempt to see the inscriptions without raising suspicion. The first house I checked belonged to the person whom we had seen when we first arrived. I didn't have to go any farther. The name was very well known to me. He was an individual whose illicit fishing behavior I had been long aware of. In ten years I had never quite had the opportunity to verify the many rumors of his poaching activities, but maybe this was the day. He was notorious in Itasca County not only for harvesting over-limits of all species of fish but also particularly for the illegal taking of large northern pike by any means necessary. This was far beyond a person of interest; he was a trophy for my book! Seven years earlier, a neighboring officer and I spent three days watching this person's fish shelter after observing a gill net set beneath his house in 30 feet of water. A gill net is another piece of equipment off limits for the taking of game fish. The net was attached to a pulley 100 feet from the house so it could be retrieved and reset immediately after removing the fish. This particular lake was known for its very large northern pike, so it was a perfect place for this type of crime. We must have been detected either by sight or foot prints in the snow because we were unsuccessful in apprehending him at that time.

I had hopes that this would be different. Being aware of his methods, I was sure that whatever he was doing in that house was most likely illegal. It was a game to him. I doubt if he was able to enjoy fishing at all unless he used an illegal method or unlawful piece of equipment. This was his motivation. If a fish wasn't worth taking illegally, it wasn't worth taking at all. This is not an uncommon attitude among some of the poaching public and is even recognized as a psychological factor explaining why some folks break the resource rules. In scientific terms, it's called the Transactional Analysis Theory, suggesting that some people poach because of the gratification it offers as a game or diversion to outwit the game warden.

The difficulty with catching a guy like this is that you have to catch him in the act. This could mean the difference of a few seconds. That's why it was necessary for me to approach his shelter in total silence and without being seen. Now, in the afternoon on a bright sunny day with two feet of snow and 100 yards from the closest shoreline, I felt my chances were slim to none. But I knew that I might never have a chance like this again, and if nothing else, I thought maybe I could put the fear of God into him to change his behavior. I hadn't observed anything wrong but was just going on instinct. Let's see. One hundred yards. Not a bad crawl if I can keep low. I just have to take it slow, very slow. If he steps out of the house for any reason, I have to be almost invisible. Without my white suit, I knew this was going to be tough. As I started through the snow on my belly, thoughts of my days in the Army came shivering back. I never thought the low-crawl would be useful again, but here I was, plowing through 2 feet of frozen precipitation, one arm and the opposite leg in unison while a white blanket of snow was sliding over the top of my hat. I had to slowly tunnel to the base of his house while peering through the crust to stay the course direction. The crystals were now sliding down my back through a break in my jacket collar. The adrenalin was pumping, and I put myself in his shoes when I would burst into the house, unannounced and say, "Game Warden. How are you today? Just checking licenses," and then observing whatever dastardly thing I could see in the darkness with my tiny, restricted pupils.

Well, the outcome was a few minutes away yet. I had another 20 yards, and I was now within ear range. Sitting in a shelter, one can hear the slightest movement, especially when you're attentive to it. Five more yards, four, two . . . now's my chance. I could reach out and touch the corner of his fish house. Just as I was ready to spring to a ready stance, the door flew open, and in all his ugly splendor, there stood "the man." Of course, there I was "the warden" lying at his heels. In the same instant, the door slammed shut and banging motions could be heard going on inside. I said to myself, "Oh no, I've got to get in the house, now!!" I jumped to my feet, trying to remain as steady as my cold cramped legs would allow, grabbed the door handle and flung it open. My eyes didn't adjust quickly enough for me to see much other than the light radiating from the open spear hole. His back was to me, so I had to force my head around his side to see anything that looked improper. There they were—two dripping decoys with treble hooks attached dangling from lines swinging 2 feet above the open water. Sitting in one corner was a spear. The law does not allow fishing with any type of a hook and having a spear in the house at the same time. The spear must be placed outside if you are angling. The problem here was that the hooks were out of the water by the time

I could focus. No doubt of his intent and no doubt the spear-injured lake trout was caused by this gentleman, but and a big "but," did what I observe constitute enough evidence to pass in court. Circumstantially, probably! Direct evidence, which is what would be needed in a misdemeanor case such as this, no! In other words, was what I saw enough to justify a rock-solid case before a judge or jury? As much as I would have liked to issue a summons, I couldn't. I did not see the hooks in the water, and that was the one observable fact I needed. **I had to let him go!** I certainly didn't want to arrest a guy with his reputation and lose, to the delight of his fishing cronies. I would take no chances. Another day maybe. There was not much conversation that afternoon. He knew . . . and maybe that's what really mattered.

The Snow Mole Strikes Again

It was a very cold, below-zero day in March. Traveling the remote roads at 11:00 p.m. looking for fishing activity could sometimes be uneventful. The crappie is a most sought-after fish all year but especially after the regular northern and walleye season has closed. Some diehards will brave the late-night cold and angle for these panfish in the deeper waters of the more secluded lakes. This particular evening I saw a faint light glowing far out in the middle of a small lake about 20 miles north of Deer River. I knew this as a lake with large crappies, so I thought investigating this small light was in order. Driving around the shore searching for the closest access to the rays, I saw through my night binoculars two people standing in a small circle of light surrounded by total blackness. No doubt they were fishing, and I suspected them of nothing illegal. But why not surprise them?! I thought that if they had any bad intentions they could certainly hide or destroy the evidence if I just walked out to them. So, I would sneak out to them and announce my arrival much closer as I looked for anything out of the ordinary. Most likely I would greet them, check their licenses and wish them well. This is also a great way of deterring future illegal behavior.

After parking my truck on an old forest road, I poked my way through a dark cedar swamp and finally slithered my way onto the deep snow at the edge of the lake. The light appeared to be about 150 yards away. It was a clear, cold, starry but moonless night.

Sounds were very detectable, so I would have to stay almost silent on my snowy journey. Once again, walking was not an option as I wanted to stay as low and invisible as possible. The crawling took forever. I underestimated the distance, which can be easily done at night, and I wound up exhausted about half way. By then I wasn't cold, but the thought of falling asleep crossed my mind, which wouldn't have been good at 10 below zero. Finally my energy level improved, and I made the final crawl to the edge of the circle of light. Now 30 feet from the two standing people, I could see what they were doing. They were fishing all right, but they were using too many lines. They were breaking the law allowing two lines per person by using seven lines between them. Not a huge violation but a violation none-theless and a mental reward for my aching arms. The trip was going to be worth it!

What approach would I take? I could sit and listen and maybe get more information, or I could just get up, walk over between them and stand there until they noticed me. Both men were pretty intent on their fishing, so slowly coming out of the darkness and trying to keep their backs to me would be inter-esting . . . OK, fun. I enjoyed surprising violators, so what bet-ter conditions than these? I was surprised myself on how long I had to wait before one of them noticed me—2 feet away. He actually looked at my feet and thought I was his buddy until he looked the other direction, looked back at me, jumped back and in an extraordinary burst of primordial panic shrieked, "What the hell . . . who are you?!!"

"I'm the local warden and just wonder how fishing is tonight?"

"Jeez, you scared the crap out of me."

I lied and said, "Didn't mean to. Just walked out to check your licenses. You do have licenses, don't you?" Well, now we had another problem. One had no license.

"Just thought I'd take a chance," he said.

"Not your only problem. Got extra lines too. Where's your fish?"

They showed me a couple of fish, way under their limit. The fella with no license looked familiar, and I had him produce a driver's license for ID. I was right! He was a character I had encountered earlier that fall at the access on this same lake. I had caught him shining deer. It's true that a small percentage of the sportsmen commit the most violations. As with any type of law enforcement, officers tend to see the same folks over and over again.

His last statement after the summonses were written was, "Do you always come up on people that way?"

I couldn't resist. "Only the guilty ones, sir. Have a good evening."

TWO

The Shining Fields

Taking deer with an artificial light or "shining" is considered a major game violation everywhere in this country. The act of shooting a wild animal while pointing a spotlight or headlights at its eyes to immobilize the creature constitutes the embodiment of big game poaching. Fair chase, the spirit and foundation of legal hunting, is totally compromised, thereby allowing the greed factor to govern. I've always considered the deer shiner to be the worst kind of poacher. Most of them with whom I've had contact were lazy and unable to grasp the basic elements of what true sport hunting is all about. Usually compounding these folks' lack of ethical behavior was alcohol. Drinking was involved in almost every deer shining contact I've ever witnessed. The following accounts were no exception.

I feel I would be remiss if I didn't expound on the first deer shining case I had the opportunity to charge in Itasca County. Like any new job, the first encounters can sometimes be the most memorable. No exception in this case!

Being generally unfamiliar with my new patrol area, I more or less picked a random spot to set up the night before the opening of deer season. Undetectable surveillance—sitting in a hidden patrol vehicle—was theoretically the best method to snag preseason poachers who would cheat on legitimate sportsmen by trying to take a deer with a spotlight or in their headlights, thus eliminating the effort of having to stalk the prey or compete with their fellow hunters the next morning. This kind of person has a twisted notion of what hunting is all about. Getting the meat is the top priority. They're lazy . . . and discharging firearms at night is potentially hazardous to everyone around them!

Around midnight, I pointed south toward the Splithand Lakes area and backed about 20 feet into a narrow trail on the north end of a large, rolling field. Seemed to me like a logical spot, next to 80 acres of alfalfa scattered with unsuspecting feeding deer. I knew it was the proverbial "shot in the dark" considering the vast number of locations from which to choose. Feeling comfortable with my choice, my civilian partner and I settled back for a long evening and poured cups of coffee to keep us alert. The whole setup reminded me somewhat of duck hunting from a blind; a waiting game, except it was totally dark and people were the prey.

I had just taken my first sip of the hot brew when lights approached from the north. No matter how many times I've been in this same situation, I just automatically get nervous and jumpy. "Here comes a vehicle," I announced to my partner. "Watch it close when he goes by. We'll try to determine its intent." I was so on edge already that I tossed my full cup of coffee out my driver's window. Problem was, I had never rolled down the window! The steam from the hot liquid on the cold glass instantly fogged the windshield as the headlights passed slowly by. "This might be a good one," I whispered to my assistant as I hurriedly wiped the inside glass with my dripping left hand. "OK, They're going exceptionally slow. We'll get right on their tail."

With lights off, I pulled out directly behind the car's taillights, using them as guidance. I assumed we'd know what his intentions were in minutes when we got to the edge of the field.

The brake lights lit up as the sedan took a hard left and headed directly toward a rise in the middle of the field. We were now tailing the car across the cut alfalfa to the top of the hill where it came to a complete stop. I quietly stepped out to look and listen. Within ten seconds, an ear-splitting CRACK-BOOM!! cut the still night air. The 2-foot yellow flame from the rifle barrel lit up the darkness behind the car's headlights. It was a strategically placed shot, dropping the deer instantly to the wet grass. "Just stay quiet," I instructed my partner. "We'll wait until they stop to pick up the critter. Then we'll take em."

By the movement seen through the back window, there appeared to be at least one other person in the vehicle. After the driver placed his rifle back inside, the car took off over the hill, down the slope and right past the dead buck. "They're going to come back later," I hollered. "We've got to get in front of them. We're going to back up and stop them when they come off the other end of the field." I did my best in the dark to back up all the way to the main road until I could see where they were going to come out. Just as their headlights shone on our bumper, we engaged the red lights. Thankfully the four-door sedan stopped. As we approached the driver's door, I noticed three heads inside. "C'mon out, fellas. You're all under arrest for deer shining. Just move in front of the lights," I directed.

To my amazement and relief, they offered absolutely no resistance, doing exactly what I ordered. The three men were shocked and shaking so violently that taking control was a simple task—one of the few cases where alcohol was not a factor.

Here's the most disappointing issue on this one. The two passengers turned out to be the shooter's teenage son and his son's young friend. What an example to pass on to the next generation! But this situation clearly reflects the core and origin of most poaching—it's a mode of conduct that's passed on from grandfather to father to son. Education is the only means by which to sever such traditional, hand-me-down behavior. I was pleased to witness the sentencing of the two boys to an eight-week, State sponsored "Advance Hunter Education Class."

The following year, still having much to learn about the elements of catching poachers, I pulled up on a hill overlooking broad fields on both sides and parked for a night of potentially exciting surveillance. Motivated by last year's success, I maneuvered my patrol unit into a perfect position to observe activity from all directions. "This is even better than last year," I thought. "Got a good civilian partner, a bag of food and a perfect natural observation platform. It's just a matter of time."

Out onto the hood we climbed. Lying on the car in sleeping bags thrown over the warm engine compartment was a traditional game warden posture for listening and observing. Sound can be detected miles away on such still evenings, and the rising warmth from the motor kept us cozy and contented. A perfect setting. Again, it was just a matter of time!

However, due to some of my earlier experiences, I was never 100 percent satisfied. Even that early in my career, I was beginning to become suspicious whenever things appeared to be too totally ideal. But I pretty much put that out of my mind as I lay there under the stars listening to the distant traffic on Highway 6.

Atypically, there was little activity all night until an hour before sunrise. Finally, though, the searching beam from a spotlight probed the large field to our south . . . and it was slowly moving our way. This was a sure thing. All we needed now was to find a gun in the vehicle and the illegal act of shining would have been committed. I was getting nervous again! I started the engine and waited. They would be passing right below us and all we would have to do was pull in behind and hit the red lights at the intersection a half mile to the north.

After six hours of coffee and waiting, I started to shake. Sometimes the anticipation is so overwhelming it makes one think too far ahead; in my mind, I already had this outfit wrapped up and the culprits in jail.

Back to reality, there they go, right by us. I put the lever in drive and tromped on the gas pedal. The wheels spun and the engine revved . . . and there we sat. The darn thing never budged. "What the heck is going on!" I shouted in total frustration. "They're getting away! What's the problem? Let's get out and take a look. How can the wheels be turning and we're not moving?"

And there we were, high and dry and completely at the mercy of "the rock." That is, a considerable boulder upon which the oil pan had run aground when I had parked earlier in the evening. We were stuck good, our rear tires elevated high enough off the ground to eliminate any chance of traction. Our spirits also bottomed out when we realized we would have to call a wrecker. We had just wasted seven hours of prime time deer poaching surveillance, a once-a-year opportunity, because of my unlucky choice of parking spots. They'll never know how lucky they were. But I bet the same outfit would be back next year—and I'd be sure not to dock on the rock.

The apprehension of each and every deer shiner possessed its own special character and intriguing trail of events. Always remember that drinking was a great motivator in most of them. I doubt if many of those involved would have pursued this night-sport without a couple shots of liquid reinforcement.

While working with Officer Tim about 2:00 a.m. in central Itasca County, we spotted a "slow mover" traveling south on County Road 8. We pulled in "black" behind them and continued the slow-follow for at least ten miles. No spotlight rays were ever cast, but the erratic driving shone the headlights into the ditches on each side of the road, raising a question of if we had a drunk, a deer shiner, or both, in front of us.

"Let's just keep following them," I told Tim. "Eventually there'll be a deer in their headlights and that should tell the tale." Normally there are deer all over this road that time of the morning, but not so that night, so we continued to stay on their tail.

An upcoming "T" would tell us more. If they took a right, they were most likely going home. A left meant they were starting to backtrack, eventually completing a large circular route. They took a left! They were definitely looking for something, and by now we surmised that a firearm was on board.

We had gone about 15 miles when their brake lights came on and the car came to a complete stop at a 45 degree angle, its headlights illuminating an open meadow. As I put our unit into park, Tim slowly emerged from the passenger side crawling on hands and knees up to the car's right rear passenger door. I glanced at the lit-up field. What appeared to be a large doe deer was standing sideways, frozen by the rays, its reflective eyes staring straight at us. I wasn't quite sure of Tim's next move as I very delicately and cautiously exited the driver's side and stood motionless. I waited for the eventual "crack" of the rifle.

Instead, suddenly I heard a mixture of struggling and grunting noises, ending with Tim's summoning, "Over here, Tom. We got 'em!" I ran the 10 feet separating the two vehicles and saw Tim holding a lever-action rifle high over his head shouting, "Got their gun. Why don't you grab the driver? I'll take care of this guy."

The middle-aged driver was no problem; he was in a kind of trance and only able to mumble a "Yes, sir" after I told him to get out of his car. He was scared but far less so than the passenger. An aroma in the air, besides the alcohol, indicated that the shooter had lost more than his gun. He could barely stand up as we repositioned both of them in front of the headlights.

It seems that after Tim crept to the side of the car, a rifle barrel was poked out of the window. Tim just reached up, grabbed the barrel and jerked the gun right out of the man's hands, most likely just seconds before a shot. Just imagine yourself in that same seat, a deer in your sights and suddenly two hands emerge from the darkness, instantly relieving you of your weapon. Now there's a heart stopper!! There's a lot to be said about the element of surprise.

"Good job, Tim. Two more for the books!" I declared. "You get an extra star for that move." It turned out these two were career poachers of deer—and probably everything else that ran or swam—with little comment about their capture. Both names were well known to us, one with a prior record of poaching. A trip to the jail and then returning to secure the bad guys' car allowed us to admire a beautiful sunrise. Another 12 hours and we'd be back at it again.

A few minutes after midnight the phone call jolted me out of bed. "Tom, something you might want to take a look at. Meet Wally at Highways 17 and 169," the dispatcher relayed. "He's holding some deer shiners for you."

Twenty minutes later, I arrived at the scene of a deputy's squad car parked at an angle in front of an older model station wagon. There was a cuffed man and a young woman standing near the front bumper and looking at the ground.

"What's up, Wally?"

"Answered one of your calls on some shooting out here and ran into this outfit throwing a spotlight out the window. Looking in the back, they've been successful. I think they need to be talked to. I wouldn't doubt there's more deer involved."

Under a mattress in the back of the station wagon were two freshly killed undressed deer. A loaded lever action 30-30 rifle

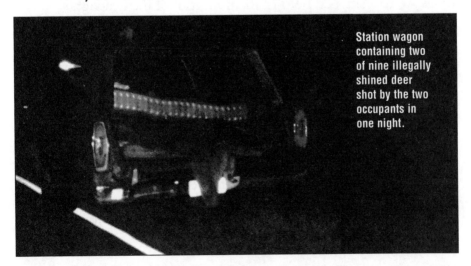

Station wagon containing two of nine illegally shined deer shot by the two occupants in one night.

was lying in the front seat next to a handheld plugged-in spotlight. It was time for interrogation!

Though both had been drinking, the young lady was more cooperative than her boyfriend, so she was who I grilled the most. Evasive at first, she finally admitted that these two weren't the only deer they had killed that night. There were many more!

She eventually concluded that cooperating with us was in her best interest and admitted that their night hunting had begun hours before. We also learned that a previous trip had been made back to their residence this same evening with other deer carcasses.

After the interview, our female poacher helped retrace their killing route. This led to the discovery of five more deer they had shot but failed to retrieve; the deer hadn't dropped immediately and had stumbled into the woods before they died. She said they didn't want to take the extra time to search for them—they just left them to rot.

Her boyfriend continued to be uncooperative, so we dropped him off at the jail for processing on our way to a small town east of Grand Rapids. Wally and I were given consent to enter a residence that was a converted movie house. Hanging from an ornate chandelier in the center of a large room was a freshly killed buck, field dressed and ready for butchering. A chest freezer in an adjacent room yielded a box of semi-frozen packages, all containing fresh venison. Total count—nine illegal deer—in one night! These two exhibited the most disgusting form of contempt for the laws and our wildlife resources. Not only did they indiscriminately shoot the deer under conditions when they are most vulnerable, but they had no qualms about wasting the animals. Theirs was the worst form of exploitation.

Yes, there were penalties assessed. Fifteen days in jail and a $500 fine for each person. An adequate punishment and deterrent for this degree of assault on our wildlife? In my opinion, a higher penalty would have sent a stronger message to those people intent on this type of behavior.

THREE
The Open-Door Policy

T he annual pastime of filching a few fish during the spring spawning run seems to have steadily declined since the early '90s. Not that game fish aren't still being taken out of season in the local rivers and creeks, but the volume of incidents is probably as low as it's ever been, most likely due to erosion of poaching traditions and our youth having their plates full of other pursuits. The vulnerability of our fish during their spawning seasons hasn't changed, and many of the locations that were seriously violated over the years continue to produce heavy fish runs. Protection of spawning fish continues to be a priority, but on the whole, fewer enforcement hours are now expended on this class of violation.

I have always claimed and continue to profess that spring work comprised some of the most wild and outrageous events I've had the good fortune or misfortune to experience during my tenure. That ominous combination of alcohol, darkness and the foolishness of youth were the ingredients for satisfying bad intentions. Spearing and hoisting a fresh meal out of a cold creek was another exciting diversion that presented itself at that time of year.

Officer Duane and I had little doubt something memorable would come to pass during the next two evenings of work. Duane had volunteered to give me a hand on my fish run enforcement for a weekend and knew from past experience that working in Itasca County normally generated some pretty significant action. We had reined in much of the illegal activity on a well-known little creek south of Grand Rapids, so we headed north to try our luck at another site.

With thermoses of coffee and enough groceries to last until sunrise, as daylight ebbed we maneuvered our vehicles through the parking lot of a bait shop and backed behind the north corner of the building. I didn't notify the owner, knowing he wouldn't care if we used his property as a surveillance position. He was a bona fide supporter of enforcement and most likely would have brought us goodies if he knew we were nearby. Our plan was to observe vehicular activity or other goings-on at a small stream flowing under State Highway 38 about a quarter mile south of us. This tiny trickle of water supplied a flow adequate to draw small northern pike out of a connected lake 50 yards to the east. The little creek was virtually unnoticeable at other times of the year, but during spring flood conditions, it created a perfect northern pike spawning site. The locals were well aware of its potential to yield buckets of mini-northern pike and of the presence of a culvert under the highway that blocked many of the struggling fish from going any farther upstream. This formed a pool from which the unsuspecting little pike could be easily plucked by hand or with a spear.

The highway traffic dwindled as the evening hours passed into the next day. We were on the lookout for the one indisputable sign that there might be interest in our quarry—the intermittent display of vehicle brakelights. Just after midnight, a northbound pickup slowed to a stop next to the culvert and just as quickly speeded up past our hiding place.

"They probably dropped somebody off," Duane commented. "Let's wait awhile."

My experienced partner was right on. Within five minutes, the same truck returned, cruising southbound with its brakelights illuminating the road as it stopped next to the creek. Our binoculars picked up the interior cab light for a split second and observed the noisy truck speed south toward town. "Let's go. You drive," Duane hollered. "We're going to have to step on it."

As I steered Duane's four-wheel-drive out of the lot and accelerated down the blacktop, we prepared ourselves for a conventional, "reasonable suspicion" stop from the rear. We caught up to the two occupants within a mile and a half and pulled alongside with red lights flashing and siren blaring. Incredibly, the vehicle refused to slow down let alone pull over. As I held our parallel position at 50 miles per hour in the opposite lane, Duane rolled down the passenger window and shouted, "Game wardens! Slow down, pull over . . . now!!"

One more time he howled, "Hold up! Stop! Pull over!"

At last, the perpetrators appeared to get the message, and their truck slowly pulled over and stopped along the narrow shoulder. "I'll cut'em off and park in front," I told Duane.

"Good! I'll get out now," Duane declared as he jumped from the cab into the blackness.

With our passenger door still open, I slammed the shift lever into park and exited my side. As I ran around our rear bumper, Duane was taking charge of the operator at the driver's door. I circled around the rear to the passenger side and grabbed the door handle. It was locked.

"Open up," I demanded. "Game Warden."

It wasn't five seconds before the rear wheels of the truck spun gravel into the air, accelerating the unit directly forward, smashing, BANG, into the open passenger door of our patrol vehicle and continuing its high-speed southbound flight attempt. "Let's go," yelled my normally unruffled partner. "Get after them!"

As I hurled my butt into the driver's seat, I noticed Duane was already sitting in an aggressive posture shouting, "Let's go. We'll get 'em."

It was quite a positive response from my pumped co-worker, considering he now had no door handle to hang on to . . . as a matter of fact, there was no door. The force of the sideswiping escape had twisted the hinges completely around, forcing the door to permanently fasten itself to the front fender. Basically, the only thing between Duane's rigid form and the passing asphalt was the cool night air as I gathered speed for the second time in pursuit of two suspects who had chosen to up the ante. We were now dealing with a fleeing case which computes to no less than a gross misdemeanor . . . all this for a couple of hammer-handle northerns . . . we assumed!

Doorless as he was, Duane was running the show. "Pull up alongside again and I'll try to persuade them to stop," he shouted above the engine's roar. This time Duane didn't have to roll down his window. There was nothing to shield his bellowing roar: "Pull it over, boys. It's all done. Just pull over."

To my amazement, they did. And we did—directly behind them into a driveway. Since Duane had no door to open, he was out and rapidly closing the gap on the passenger. Yup, they decided to make a foot race out of it. My target was the driver who squirted down the dark gravel with me in pursuit. A 20-yard sprint and a half-tackle netted my man. When I looked up, Duane, an imposing figure to say the least, was holding his fish thief off the ground by the scruff of the neck.

"How ya doin, Tom?" he casually asked as he contemplated both of us stretched out on the ground.

"OK, big guy," I muttered. "I think things are under control here."

We decided to apply some hand restraints to squelch a possible third pursuit. As everyone gained his composure back at the trucks, the two young fish bandits were advised of their legal rights and their truck was searched. A small bag of pickling northerns was found to be the loot responsible for this out-ofproportion state of affairs. After we left the jail, Duane remarked, "What are we doing tomorrow evening?"

"Same thing if you're willing," I responded with a gratifying sigh. "We can use my truck tomorrow night!"

That evening with my patrol unit yet unscathed, we backed up into the same hideout next to our favorite bait shop and cut the lights. A stock of small fish were on hand again in the creek, so we hoped to repeat last evening's success minus the pursuit fiasco.

Again it was just after midnight when northbound head-lights slowed to a stop next to our favored culvert. This time there appeared to be activity outside the car for quite a while. Over five minutes elapsed before it sped north past our probing stares. Just after the little car passed by our concealed position, we slid in dark behind the Volkswagen and followed the tiny taillights to the next county road where the car took an abrupt left. "Might as well take'em now, Duane. Pretty safe area. Let's see what they've got."

"Sounds good to me," Duane responded. "Just pull up along-side and hit the lights."

Instantly the little car reacted with a feeble surge of its air-cooled motor as we pulled alongside. The whole scene seemed a replay of the previous night's events.

"Not again," I thought. "Just what we need: another chase over a silly little fish."

Duane was replaying last night's script, gesturing and screaming at the driver to pull over. Again, the same routine as experienced 24 hours earlier—a refusal to obey our simple instructions. Maybe everybody around here missed the class on the significance of flashing red lights. Whatever the reason, we had another chase going, this time, on a narrow county road with upcoming curves.

"They have no intention of stopping," hollered Duane. "Why don't you just give them a tap on the left bumper. That'll get their attention. Looks like she's trying to get the sack out the passenger window."

As I slowly urged our truck to the right, the scratch of metal on metal preceded the inevitable soft landing of the Bug into the shallow grassy ditch. Duane exited instantly and took control of the pike poachers.

"They aren't going to run this time," I reflected as I totally blocked any avenue of escape.

"What do we have here?" Duane inquired as he pulled a gunnysack filled with tiny pike from the passenger floor of the small vehicle. "Seems like you've got a honey-hole here. We're 100 percent."

Apparently the female passenger was attempting to get the fish out the passenger door window but was unable to get the glass down far enough to slide the bag through. This malfunctioning window allowed us to secure the evidence necessary to charge each with taking game fish before season.

The small fines assessed hopefully would be a deterrent for future violations by this pair. Risking their lives, risking the lives of others–some forms of poaching are parts of a lifestyle fraught with bad decisions.

FOUR

The Eager Beavers

History says if it wasn't for the beaver, the opening and taming of the west would have taken place much later than it did. Minnesota's own first exploration was triggered by the abundance and value of America's biggest rodent. The most sought after animal ever trapped in North America, trapping beaver provided much of the incentive whereby Europeans would come to settle these wild lands in the 17th and 18th centuries.

Every resource is finite, and the beaver was no exception. As vast expanses of their habitat were altered and the European demand for beaver pelts continued to increase, beaver populations decreased to a point that closed seasons were imposed in Minnesota in the early part of the 20th century. In a few places, the sighting of a beaver would even make local news.

One way to get a conversation started among a group of trappers and former trappers is to bring up the fluctuations in beaver prices witnessed over the last half century. They'll all tell you the high prices they received for a "blanket"-grade beaver hide in the '60s. Then they will discuss the rise and fall since then of all furbearer values and how today it isn't worth the effort to trap the beaver, or most anything else, for profit. Everyone will admit this dilemma is totally dependent on the overseas demand. Folks around the world just aren't wearing natural animal furs as they used to.

Itasca County had, and still has, lots of beaver. Its thousand lakes and vast river network create the perfect habitat for this prolific critter. It eventually became a nuisance in many areas by damming up creeks and waterways and by causing flooding problems.

The opening of beaver season in late October was eagerly anticipated by local trappers. Until the mid-'80s, a good trapper could make thousands of extra dollars, and a few could even support themselves on their trapping income. Some, however, would start trapping before the season opened, thus getting a jump on their legal competition!

I knew of an area just east of the Prairie River that was dotted with small sloughs, each with at least one beaver house and the scrubby, terrestrial plant life that was favorable for beaver habitation. My previous visits led me to conclude that if there ever was a remote, nearly inaccessible area ripe for illegal activity, this was it.

I approached the swampy area from the west, sliding down a steep railroad grade into a watery patchwork of bogs and slough grass. As I slogged and stumbled my way a hundred yards toward a higher patch of ground, I was certain I detected a definite human sound a few hundred yards in front of me. It seemed to be more of an intermittent, muted garble than a distinct voice, but it was for sure made by a person or persons. "There's only one reason somebody would be back here," I thought. "It only can be for trapping. Nobody in his right mind would be navigating this awful, flooded jungle for any other reason than to pursue beaver."

Crawling to a viewing spot on a slight hill, I scanned with my binoculars as I stood among the thick alder branches. I caught a glimpse of two human forms both hunched over the shallow water near an old beaver house. I continued my surveillance until I was satisfied that both of the young men were partaking in "before season" trapping. They were setting a type of body-gripping trap called a Conibear. This particular trap causes an instant death when triggered and is considered the most humane of devices used to harvest furbearing animals.

Now, I had to devise a strategy. Attempting to get closer without detection was certainly necessary, but having experienced this same situation so many times before, the odds were extremely high the culprits would sense my presence and hightail it out of there. Unless there were unforeseen expressions of instant repentance by these two for exploiting the resource and taking advantage of legal trappers, I was going to be in a foot chase . . . in hip-boots!

I began creeping through dense willow growth and soggy tufts of grass; the closer I could get, the less distance I would have to make up if a chase occurred. I was within 50 feet before the two whirled around toward the sounds of my approach, glared at my form for a split second, and in unison dashed off eastbound. The direction of their abrupt flight led eastward through a 3-mile stretch of birch, aspen and pines. I remember thinking, "If they choose to continue on this bearing, I'll most likely lose sight of them and wind up with little to show for my exhaustion." I could see immediately that I was losing ground; they were younger and could run faster.

I had one tool left . . . my portable radio. While I jogged along, I shouted into the mike: "K-car to Itasca Sheriff's Office . . . K-car to Itasca SO. Can you copy?" Just after I lost sight of the two for the last time, amazingly, the Sheriff's office answered, "Yeah. Go ahead."

"I'm in a foot chase with a couple of young guys in camouflage jackets in the woods north of Highway 169 heading toward Coleraine. If you've got a car anywhere near, I'd appreciate some help."

"See what we can do. How far east are you ?" shouted the dispatcher.

"Figured I've been after them about 20 minutes. I would guess a mile from town. I'll get back to you in a few minutes."

Now completely out of wind, I more walked than ran. I assumed they were still ahead of me and would eventually come out near the cemetery. With my radio in hand, I continued for another mile until I heard the radio squawking. "Tom, can you copy?"

"Go ahead," I panted.

"This is Joe. I'll meet you at the cemetery."

"OK," I answered. "About five minutes." I wasn't quite sure what was happening until I burst out of the woods onto the green grass. To my right was an unmarked squad car with a deputy standing next to the driver's door.

"You can take it easy," shouted Joe. "I've got em!"

As I strolled up to the sheriff's sedan, I saw the backs of two heads through the rear window. "How did you accomplish this?" I asked in amazement.

"I was just down the road when I got your call. From your description, I figured they'd have to come out in the open sometime, so I parked along the driveway here. It wasn't five minutes and these two guys walked out of the woods, came over to my car and asked for a ride. They obviously had no idea that I was a deputy so I said, 'Sure . . . get in!' And that's the first time they saw the uniform—and the cage in the back. 'You might as well have a seat, I told them. I think the game warden wants to talk to you.'"

"You've just turned a discouraging morning into a very worthwhile day," I responded with admiration. "Thanks for the help. I at least owe you coffee!"

It was a warm and sunny early April spring morning following a night when the temperature hadn't dipped below freezing. Only patches of snow remained in the shaded areas of the woods, and the water levels in the local creeks were at their highest points of the season.

I was just walking out the door to begin a day's patrol when the phone rang. The fellow calling wanted any information I might have on the ownership of some land adjacent to his hunting shack in northern Itasca County. It seemed that some beaver trappers had left some skinned carcasses on his property, and the remains appeared to have originated at this site. I told him I was unaware of any landowner names in that particular area but did know of a trapper who regularly trapped beaver near there and who might know other trappers in the region. "In fact," I told him, "I'll stop by his residence on my way north this morning and see if he's home. I'll get back to you."

Only 15 minutes from my home, I drove up the trapper's muddy driveway and parked next to his pickup. Glancing in the box, I could see patches of blood and hair that I assumed were remnants of beaver trapped over the last five months. The screen door on the attached entryway to the mobile home was partially open, so I walked in and rapped on the inside door. "C'mon in," a loud voice responded. "Door's open." I turned the knob and pushed the door into the kitchen area where my contact was sitting at a table a few feet away. As he casually glanced up, I instantly knew I was not the person he was expecting to walk through the door. Our eyes made direct contact, his stare taking up a guise of forced self-control. "Oh . . . hi, Tom. What's going on?"

"Looks like I'm going to have to ask you that. What do we have here?" I answered, surprised. Lying on the table were two otters in various stages of skinning, and on the floor next to the refrigerator was a totally skinned otter carcass. "Unless you can show me a tag for those critters, it looks like we have a problem here," I asserted. "How about dropping the knife on the floor, too."

It wasn't that this guy was dangerous, but no one can predict a person's reactions when confronted so abruptly, especially on one's own property. "You know, if you would have just called, you wouldn't be in this mess," I said.

Many trappers like this fellow find themselves in an ethical dilemma when trapping beaver in the spring. Sometimes an otter is trapped accidentally and must be turned in to the local game warden since the season for otter is only open in the fall of the year. The problem arises because an otter hide can be worth four times the value of a beaver. The decision then focuses on the "greed factor" issue: Am I obliged to turn them over to the State, or should I keep them and pass them off as legal animals next season? The temptation always resides in the profit . . . and this situation was a perfect example; trapping is hard work, and the chance of getting caught is almost nil. Finding these illegal otters was an extraordinary event!

Two freshly skinned illegally taken spring otter hides and one otter carcass.

Illegal possession of certain furbearing animals—otter, marten, fisher, bobcat—is considered a gross misdemeanor which dictates larger penalties than most game and fish violations. Knowing his past history, I had no qualms about charging this individual. As the conversation became less strained and he accepted his fate, I asked him the questions for which I had originally stopped. He was cooperative and did in fact supply me with the information I needed to help the earlier caller. I wish to emphasize that many poachers are otherwise pretty good citizens!

FIVE
The Gross Overlimiters

Apprehending people taking huge over-limits of fish is exceptionally rare during most game wardens' careers. Folks who are intent on "hogging" our fish in great numbers can get by for years, and in most cases, all of their fishing lives, with little fear of getting caught with the goods. Anyone who does a minimal amount of planning prior to transporting the contraband by-and-large has such a small chance of capture that it borders on hilarity. The main reason—not enough enforcement personnel to do the job! Arrests involving major over-limits don't just happen out of the blue. Most are products of intense investigation and years of creating personal relationships with potential tipsters. How many of these gross violations are taking place is anybody's guess, but a most disturbing fact is the relatively large number of arrests made as a result of random stops and checks. These arbitrary, hit-and-miss encounters indicate the extent of the problem. Itasca County is a prime location for this type of incident. The following cases are examples of major over-limits relating to three different species of fish.

As I drove to meet with two officers on a damp May morning, I couldn't help wondering what it might be like to take a day off and try to catch a fish myself, instead of searching for and counting someone else's fish. The first two days of the season had been excellent fishing on most lakes, resulting in long hours and numerous citations issued for over-limit possessions. As the sun peeked above the horizon, I assumed that this Monday morning might unearth more misdeeds since we would be checking an area where the fish had been biting extremely well.

As the sun cast its warming rays on the roadside grasses, the mosquitos found their way to our set-up location on a gravel road. So much so, we each grabbed our head-nets to keep from being overwhelmed by the vicious bloodsuckers. This particular driveway led to a resort on a lake where the word was out on fishing success. Our plan was to set up a small sign announcing our presence and check a few cars coming from the lake. As I looked for a good spot to place the marker, I saw a small, nondescript car heading from the resort in our direction. "Here comes a vehicle," I hollered at my partners. "Do you want to stop it?"

"We're not quite set up yet. But, whatever you think, Tom," they replied.

As I fumbled with the signposts, the little car came to a stop next to me. I assumed he thought he was required to stop, so I walked over to the driver's door. "How's fishing?" I asked. "Are you a fisherman?" "Yes, I am," he stated as he got out of his vehicle. "Do you have any fish with you?"

"Yes, sir!" he declared in a military manner. "I believe I have too many!"

I looked at this well-dressed, polite, and erect-standing gentleman and wondered if I had heard him correctly. I couldn't ever remember when a person had so quickly admitted to a violation, let alone with such an obliging and friendly attitude. I thought I was dreaming. Was this guy for real?

As I pulled my mosquito net off my head, I inquired as to the location of the fish. "They're all in the trunk. I have way too many fish!" he calmly reiterated. "Here. I'll open it for you." If there was ever going to be a "Most Courteous and Respectful Violator Award" presented, this man would be the first recipient.

"What are you, a couple over?" I asked as he reached for a large cooler in the trunk.

"Quite a bit more than that," he mumbled. "I think I may be in big trouble." I helped him pull the heavy container over the bumper, and it plopped hard onto the ground. He opened the lid—and I couldn't believe what I was peering at. The thing was three-quarters full of white, marked packages, all walleye fillets. The contents and numbers of fish inside each could be read on the paper.

Two out-of-state boats, the top boat containing an over-limit of 149 largemouth bass.

"How many fish do you have here?" I asked in amazement.

"Way too many. I'm in trouble, aren't I?"

"We'll have to count first, but yes, sir, you have a problem here."

After the final count of 186 walleyes (the limit is six), my first question after reading him the Miranda Warning was to inquire if he had caught all the fish himself and what he was planning on doing with them. "I had a little help," he said, "but as you know, the fish are really biting. You can catch as many as you want right off the dock. I'm the assistant fire chief for the Milwaukee Fire Department, if that tells you anything."

"Heck of a fry you boys were planning on having—all off Minnesota fish! You know you're going to have to pay for this."

"Yup. I'm caught, and I knew exactly what I was doing. I certainly know there are consequences."

He was so cooperative, I almost declared a "Hug a Violator Day." He did pay a substantial fine. But because of the law current at that time, no jail time and no confiscation of equipment or revocation of his fishing privileges were allowed. He could have legally fished the next day! Fortunately since March of 2003, that has changed.

The next case involved roughly the same scenario, but this time it was winter. The purpose of our road check was to monitor the fishing success of folks returning home after a weekend on Lake Winnibigoshish and the surrounding lakes. About a dozen of us had already uncovered six over-limits of perch, including a stash of fish hidden in a trailer marked "The Fishin' Mission" in large black letters on the rear panel.

About halfway into our setup, one individual with a snowmobile trailer was pulled over and checked for fish. On the trailer was a large red cargo sled packed with ice. "How was fishing?" I inquired as usual.

"Got my limit of perch. They're in the sled," he growled. "How come you guys are doing this? Don't you have anything better to do? You should all be out on the lakes where the fish are."

"Yes, sir. We'll let you go in a minute. Just got to check the sled." I bit my tongue and started moving the ice aside to get to the layer of perch.

"Got my limit of a hundred. They're right there under that top layer," the man shouted.

"Is that all you have? Any more fish under here?" I inquired further.

"Nope. Are you done now?"

Motor home freezer stuffed full of walleyes—79 over the limit

"Hold on a second . . . what's this?" As I groped to the bottom through the thick layer of ice, I felt another fish tail. A crappie. Pulling it out, I asked, "How many of these do you have?"

The man had no reply and instantly dropped his antagonistic demeanor. His head hung as he started to walk toward his vehicle. The more I poked, the more fish I could feel at the bottom of the sled. By the time we were done digging and counting, a total of 95 large crappies had been removed (15 was the limit). This was another case of greed overtaking any desire to stay within the limits of the law. If it weren't for these rare roadchecks, suspects like this would never be caught. As of this writing, the "road check," which had been used for years as a tool by enforcement to help curtail this type of behavior, has been judged unconstitutional and is no longer allowed.

This third scenario came about only because of good people doing good things. Individuals who call the authorities about game and fish violations must be given credit for taking that

extra step. Sometimes the little act of picking up a phone and putting yourself on the line as an informant is more challenging than you would think. "Do I really want to get involved? What if somebody finds out? Will it be handled professionally?" All these concerns flash through the minds of the people who are about to become what some of the public refer to as a "stoolie." All these feelings have to be overcome before the final commitment is made for the protection of the resource. It's not an easy thing . . . and wardens know this!

That's why it was so important on this particular day to reassure the person calling how I respected his decision to come forth with the information and that I would do whatever it took to protect him from any harmful effects. In this particular instance, I did not know the identity of the caller. I didn't care. I just thanked him and said I would do my best to catch the potential culprits.

Sometimes it doesn't take a lot of information. An anonymous call like this may only reveal what are now called "persons of interest." Many times that's all we need to direct us to a location or a vehicle so that further investigation can take place. In this case it was a truck pulling a unique trailer carrying two boats piggyback. Indiana plates also helped, but the trailer was the key. By the time I got to the north side of town, I spotted the southbound suspects. As they passed me in the opposite direction, I thought, "Whew, that was close. Just about missed them."

After quickly turning around, I tailed them to a spot that would be safe and adequate for an inspection—the parking lot of the local arena. I could see four heads in the crew-cab pickup as they dutifully pulled over next to a grassy lot. All four men immediately exited their vehicle and approached me with looks of bewilderment. "Hello, Officer, what seems to be the problem?" they inquired in puzzled tones.

"Game warden. Got some information that you guys have some fish on board. Is that true?" Not knowing for sure if a violation was even present, I always liked to ask them first. I figured if they said no, they wouldn't object to a search of their equipment. If they said yes, I would ask them if I could see their catch. You see, I really had to rely on their consent to let me proceed any further. An anonymous call is not enough probable cause to allow a search without a warrant.

"We have no fish," the driver explained. "We just come up here to 'catch and release.' You have the greatest bass fishing in this area. We just love coming here. This is our third trip this summer, and we've been coming on and off for over nine years. We don't have bass like this back in Indiana."

You had to be there to appreciate the full extent to which these guys exuded their pride. Each of them was what I call "patched up." Their hats and jackets were filled with patches representing all the different bass clubs they had either belonged to or with whom they had some connection. As I looked over the various insignias, they were quick to acknowledge their fishing prowess and the fact that they were considered "professionals" back home. "Wow," I remarked. "You boys are really into it. Whatdaya say I have a look in your boats, just for curiosity. If nothing else, I'll get a chance to see some of your equipment. Maybe I can learn something."

I had them where I wanted them. They wouldn't deny me now, even if they had fish. So I started to do my thing. The trailer carrying the two boats was a marvel of homemade engineering. I climbed into the bottom boat and rummaged through all their bags and equipment primarily looking for coolers or something that felt cold. It's amazing how much stuff can be packed into an 18-foot craft. I watched them watch me and everyone appeared relaxed and remarkably hassle-free. After 15 minutes of going through bags and boxes, I straddled the outside frame and hopped into the top boat. "Same thing up there," one of them shouted. "You won't find any fish."

I immediately raised an eyebrow and said to myself, "Whoops! Big mistake." This little comment was my first clue that my curiosity might pay off.

To me, this was really a defensive statement, a little hint of nervousness that encouraged me to finish the task. I worked my way from the stern to the bow, feeling and poking my hands into anything that might hold a fish. Finally deep in the bowels of the bow under a layer of sleeping bags I found a red cooler. This was the end of the search and the last container I would inspect. I opened the lid and felt inside. Instant cold. I lay prone and positioned myself so I could peek under the lid. The satisfaction and relief derived from witnessing what I saw at that instance is hard to match. The container was full . . . package after package of frozen fillets. "They almost had me," I thought, "but they're mine now!"

I pulled the heavy cooler from the bow and lowered it over the sides of the boats to the ground below. I watched as the fellows' demeanors succumbed to the reality of the situation. They sat on the grass, heads bowed as if readying themselves for a whipping. "Let's see exactly how many of these 'catch-and-release' bass you have here," I declared.

The final count was memorable, considering that these guys came to the area at least 25 times over the last nine years if their calculations were accurate. A total of 149 largemouth bass (legal limit of six per person). This was another example of the greed factor and of the fact that they had never been checked in all

350 crappies in a cabin freezer caught and illegally possessed by two persons.

those years. How important is enforcement visibility and occasional checks? This case is a perfect example.

Addendum: These fishermen, like the previous two, had no equipment confiscated or licenses revoked. Hopefully, the new law effective March 1, 2003, allowing for confiscation and license revocation, will help in deterring these gross violations.

SIX

The Hidden Threat

T he following narrative was written by Conservation Officer Lloyd Steen of Ray, Minnesota. Officer Steen currently patrols the Lake Kabetogama and Rainy Lake areas of far northern Minnesota along the Canadian border. I invited Lloyd to contribute one of his most memorable episodes of his career. This is his story.

I thought it was rather warm and calm for a late September day on Lake Kabetogama in northern Minnesota. I landed my 19-foot Lund patrol boat on the east shore of Tom Cod Bay, cut the motor and looked up at the overcast skies. I realized it must have been raining most of the night, as I looked down at the soft, moist, fresh fallen leaves. I didn't know it then, but that gentle rain and the wet leaves would save my life within the hour. It all started about a month earlier, when a St. Louis County deputy sheriff happened to mention to me that he had reason to believe there was a wanted man, a prison escapee, somewhere in northern St. Louis County. The deputy told me to keep my eyes and ears open for any info, and I agreed I would.

A few weeks passed, and I had just about forgotten about the escaped convict. I was going about my regular duties patrolling the remote forest roads with my truck, checking small game and archery hunters, when I saw a local landowner named Paul near his mailbox. Paul lived on a dead-end dirt road surrounded by woods, which happened to be within a mile of the Voyageurs National Park boundary. I stopped and made small talk with Paul. During our conversation, however, Paul mentioned that a strange thing had happened the other morning. He said that while exiting from his driveway onto the township road, he noticed a man in camouflage jump off the road into the ditch and lie down, as if he was trying to hide. Paul drove up and looked down at the man and asked him what he was doing. The man didn't respond but got up and just walked away. Paul continued on but thought it strange in that the man didn't appear to be a hunter and that he hadn't noticed any vehicle the man would have needed to get to such a remote spot.

It sounded strange to me also, and I wondered to myself if this could possibly be our escaped fugitive. A few days later I met with Mike, one of the local park rangers, and mentioned the new information that I had just received from Paul. I explained that it would be a good idea for him to share the info with the other rangers and that I would pass it on to the other law enforcement officers as well.

A couple more weeks went by without any further information about our mysterious man in camouflage until Ranger Mike unexpectedly came upon him while patrolling the park boundary on foot. Mike had taken a boat back into Tom Cod Bay and then walked on an old, all-terrain vehicle (ATV) trail towards its intersection with a logging road. The logging road ran south away from the park and toward the dead-end road by Paul's residence. Mike was checking the condition of the closed-to-motor-vehicle signs in the vicinity.

As Mike walked out of the woods, he saw an unarmed man dressed in camouflage with a pack on his back walking towards him. The man was stocky, about 160 pounds with short dark hair and wearing glasses. Mike guessed his age at 40 and asked him what he was doing. The man replied that he was just walking and canoeing in the park. Mike then asked for ID but the man refused. Mike was obviously suspicious of the man and convinced him to reveal the contents of his pack—canned goods of carrots, beans, peaches, etc. Mike also asked to see his canoe, but the man couldn't remember where he had placed it. The man pressed the issue that if he wasn't under arrest he was going to leave. Since Mike couldn't prove any wrongdoing, he was forced to let the man go; the man walked off toward the wooded lakeshore, and Mike headed back down the trail to his boat.

The next day Mike contacted me and gave me the play-by-play details of his contact and a physical description of the camouflaged clad hiker. Because of the proximity to Paul's residence and the similar descriptions, we agreed that this was most likely the same man. I spread the news among the local law enforcement and conservation officers. We had no more contact with the man in the next few days.

I became more curious about this possible fugitive from justice, so I contacted the St. Louis County Sheriff's Office in an attempt to get a name and better physical description. I soon learned that the fugitive whom the deputy had initially told me about had recently been captured and returned to prison. This information certainly didn't help solve the puzzle. Everyone involved so far agreed that this man acted like a fugitive from justice. Could there possibly be two? Was this a different man hiding from an arrest warrant? I would learn soon enough.

The following afternoon I ended up at the Koochiching County Law Enforcement Center. I just pulled into the lot when I got a call from Mike who asked me to call him at his office. Mike explained that he and another ranger had just returned from the area of Tom Cod Bay where they had seen the camouflaged man a week earlier. Mike said they had found the man's canoe hidden in the grass and had followed a deer trail filled with human tracks. As they followed the trail over the rock ridges a quarter mile away, they observed a deer hanging from a pole and logs on the ground arranged as if part of a camp. The rangers wisely retreated and immediately radioed me. The rangers believed that the camp was located on state or county property, not within the federal park. I told Mike I would get some additional help and meet him at his office.

I explained the information to Koochiching County Deputy Bob and suggested that this man was most likely wanted and probably had taken an illegal deer. I also believed that there was a high probability that he was living in the woods and was dangerous. Bob decided that two park rangers, a deputy sheriff and one conservation officer should be enough manpower to capture the man.

Deputy Bob and I drove to the Voyageurs National Park Ranger Station and loaded our gear into my boat. I radioed the rangers who were waiting our arrival at Tom Cod Bay. As I pulled my boat alongside the ranger's boat, I mentioned how calm and quiet it was and that we needed to land our boats at trolling speed. I eventually landed my boat on the east shore, cut my motor and jumped out onto the damp, wet leaves. After tying up the boats, the four of us walked into the woods to form a plan. We didn't know what to expect, but agreed we should plan for the worst; a wanted man who didn't want to be caught and lived in the woods was very likely armed and dangerous.

It was agreed there needed to be a point man, one who was out front of the rest. From this time on, there could be no talking, only hand signals. It was then that I noticed what we lacked for weapons. I couldn't believe that I was the only officer who was carrying a short-barreled, 12-gauge shotgun loaded with double-ought buckshot. Apparently the other officers felt confident enough just carrying their semi-auto pistols; I felt better carrying an added shotgun. I don't know why, but I volunteered to be the point man. I don't consider myself a hero, nor do I have a death wish, it was just the fact that somebody had to do it and nobody else was jumping to the front. We spread out single file and slowly melted into the deep woods from the shoreline. It was easy following the worn deer trail through the spruce, balsam and aspen trees. I crept along over the soaked leaves and wet ground, one step at a time. I crouched often and froze in place to observe for periods of time, like a deer when it senses unseen danger.

I remember thinking, "Is this even remotely what it was like being at war?" I was in high school when Viet Nam ended, and I never experienced the fears of creeping through the jungles hunting men and being hunted by them. I was very thankful for the wet leaves that masked any noise of my footsteps. It seemed like it took a long time creeping, crouching, watching and feeling my heart pounding; but then I saw the deer hanging. I backed up and motioned to the officers what I had just seen.

One of the two rangers whispered they wouldn't be going past the ridge ahead because he believed they would no longer be on federal property and didn't have jurisdiction except on federal land. I was dumbfounded, but this was no time to argue. I handed the ranger my shotgun and told him to cover Deputy Bob and me from the ridge and that we would go the rest of the way ourselves.

I continued on point, walking, creeping, watching, until I approached the hanging deer. It turned out to be a deer hide, not an entire hanging deer. The hide was obviously from a deer taken out of season due to its orange summer coat.

As I continued creeping ahead, I noticed a 4 x 6-foot-wide log structure that was also about 4 feet high. I could see hundreds of canned goods through the cracks in the logs; it was obviously some sort of food cache. Spruce and balsam trees grew tall along the ridge trail, casting shadows far ahead of the log building. Further into the trees, I suddenly saw a log cabin chinked with moss and a small window on the south side facing me. I could see straight through the window and out the north window on the opposite side. I could also see a front door on the east end.

I dropped down below the log food cache and motioned Deputy Bob to get down. We continued to watch the cabin for several minutes when suddenly I saw the camouflaged man walking toward the cabin from the north. He walked to the window and started to work on it. I could plainly see him through both windows so I motioned to Bob to get ready. I drew my pistol and hollered, "Game Warden!" Instantly the man dropped down out of sight below the window. Deputy Bob then added, "Sheriff's Office! Put your hands up!" I looked over at Bob who had his gun pointed toward the west end of the cabin. The extended wall logs plus the dark shadows of the roof and spruce trees completely concealed the man. We were at a standoff and we knew it.

As Deputy Bob continued to shout commands, I heard the very reassuring sound of a nearby ranger chambering a round into the shotgun. "Something has to be done, but what should we do now?" I pondered. "Does he have a gun?" I couldn't see if he had one when he originally came down the trail or when he was working near the window. I saw an opportunity for cover and ran across the wet leaves to the east end of the cabin. I then slowly crept along the north side until I came to the west end. The extended logs had large spaces between them where there was no moss chinking. I peeked through the cracks in the logs and saw the man hiding in the shadows of the logs with his back up against the wall. I could plainly see the man's hands, and, knowing he couldn't see me, I dashed around the logs and grabbed the suspect by pushing him up against the wall. I rapidly placed handcuffs on the man and then yelled to the other officers that it was OK. I had him.

I turned the man around and asked him his name. While looking straight at me and ignoring my questions he said, "How did you sneak up on me? If I would have heard you first, I WOULD HAVE KILLED YOU!" I looked into his staring, steely eyes and realized he was telling me the truth, and he said it so matter-of-factly. After the other officers arrived, we attempted to ID the man, but he wasn't very talkative, and he definitely wasn't going to tell us his name. Deputy Bob continued to ask questions of the man as I walked around the cabin and entered the front door. The cabin was a 10 x 16-foot structure made from aspen logs with a dirt floor. A log bed, a small table, and a bench serving as a chair were the only furniture. A small barrel stove served for heat, and a Coleman lantern and candles appeared to be his light.

Lying on top of his bed was a loaded 9-mm pistol in a holster on a belt, along with a loaded 30-30 caliber rifle. Under the bed were a compound bow and some arrows. Next to the bed was a notebook which I opened. It was a diary of his life and events over the last two years of his living and hiding from the world in this cabin. I briefly scanned the pages and decided to read more later.

I also found his wallet under the bed and was able to retrieve his Wisconsin driver's license revealing the last name of Korbenhagen. Finally I was able to put a name with this guy! I gathered up the weapons, the wallet and the diary and met with the other officers outside.

"I know who you are, Korbenhagen," I said. At this revelation of his identity, Korbenhagen suddenly began to talk. He admitted he had an outstanding warrant for his arrest in Wisconsin and that he had been living here in the woods for two years.

This concludes the account of the man's capture. What follows can only be summed up as unexpected and disheartening.

Once a person is in custody, it is then up to the criminal justice system to formally charge the defendant based on the evidence provided or to release the person within a legal time frame. We all knew that this case involved criminal behavior; for sure there were wildlife and trespassing violations in addition to the outstanding warrant. What we didn't count on was the mind-boggling twist this investigation would take.

The first odd finding, or lack of finding, was the failure to locate an outstanding warrant for the man in Minnesota or Wisconsin. After finally locating and talking to Korbenhagen's Wisconsin probation officer, we found that a warrant had indeed been issued in Korbenhagen's name, but it was only valid if he was apprehended in Wisconsin. The probation officer didn't want him back!

The diary revealed that Korbenhagen was severely burned while working as a factory worker and was fired from his job. That he hired an attorney in a lawsuit against the company and wound up choking his attorney in the courtroom for inadequately presenting his case. That he was sentenced to a year in jail (served seven months) for his assault and divorced his wife while in jail. That he fled to Minnesota after violating his probation conditions by driving his van to Voyageurs National Park after storing the vehicle in International Falls. That he existed by illegally building a log cabin and using a canoe and bicycle for transportation.

I almost felt myself feeling a little sorry for his misfortunes that led him to a life of hiding until I reminded myself that this same man only hours earlier had said he would have killed me if given the chance. He also reiterated this while I questioned him in jail . . . "You were lucky the leaves were wet and I didn't hear you first. If I had heard you first, I would have killed you."

The final blow came when the County Attorney began explaining to me that he believed I didn't have a very winnable case. He held that even though the cabin logs were stolen and that Korbenhagen was trespassing on private land, I may have violated his rights by entering the squatter's cabin without a search warrant; the diary was wrongfully obtained. Furthermore the county attorney had just lost a sexual abuse case involving criminal acts recorded in a person's private diary. The jury believed the diary to be mere fantasy in the defendant's mind instead of hard facts. He wasn't about to try a case again with the main evidence being a diary. He refused to prosecute Korbenhagen.

I related the conversation to Deputy Bob who was equally disappointed with the decision not to prosecute such a dangerous man. We knew we had no choice but to release him. I informed Korbenhagen that he was trespassing and had two days to pack up his belongings from the illegal cabin and leave the county. His seized firearms would be returned and he was free to go. Korbenhagen didn't say anything but nodded that he understood. At least this time he didn't threaten me.

A few weeks after Korbenhagen was released from jail, I returned to the empty cabin just to ensure he was really gone. It was an eerie visit, as I speculated how things perhaps could have turned out differently if I hadn't been careful and if the leaves hadn't been wet.

It took several months to let go of the disappointment of realizing that I was yet another officer who had risked his life to apprehend a fugitive, a poacher and potential murderer, only to have the legal system let him go.

I want to believe that Korbenhagen got his life straightened out after our encounter and that he returned to society to live a normal life instead of a paranoid existence in the woods. I want to believe that, but I don't.

SEVEN

The Serendipitous Live-Well

This narrative exemplifies one of the many preseason fishing infractions I've witnessed over the years. This particular incident reveals the pattern of elements that I've discovered while pursuing folks taking fish before the legal season, including, but not limited to darkness, secrecy, vigilance, suspicion, greed and a basic lack of sportsmanship.

I must qualify the significance of these types of poachers; they make up a very small segment of the overall violation totals. They certainly aren't numerous enough to affect the fish populations to any degree. So are they worth pursuing and consuming valuable time that might be otherwise spent on more critical enforcement matters? Of course they are! Let's go back to the definition of a warden's job, which is to create a fair playing field. Nobody likes a cheater, especially one who takes advantage of many people at the same time. The guy rushing the season affects everyone who invests in a license and tries to follow the rules. He knows that illegally taken fish belong to the state . . . meaning us! All legal fishermen should support game wardens going after these violators; they are stealing from YOU!

A hot fishing pond west of town was always a favorite place to relax and observe fishing activity, especially before dark. I could cozy up under my favorite tree or find a brushy bend on the shore to cover my presence and just watch. Some would call this spying. I preferred to dub this type of surveillance as an "undercover, covert, intelligence--gathering system for the purpose of neutralizing illicit fishing behavior." I suppose it doesn't matter what you call it–I thought it a good use of my time. Besides, I had been very successful over the years, especially at this location. I was hoping this stretch of luck would continue this evening.

Surveillance of this specific site required stashing my truck in the brush a half mile from the lake. I had to completely hide it from view so anyone traveling along the dead-end road would be unaware of my presence. I then traipsed through the woods to my favorite hiding spot where I could look out over the entire bay.

It was clear and rather warm for a late April afternoon. Although an hour until sunset, there were no less than five boats moving about on the calm water. Two or three fishermen in each craft could be seen casting or concentrating on their small bobbers floating on the sparkling surface. The whole scene was so ideal and pristine. It was one of those moments when the fading light and the smells of spring made time stand still.

I had such a clear and unhindered view through my 8X50 binoculars that not only could I see the registration numbers on each boat but also I could identify the facial features of most of the people. Because of my previous trips to this fishing hole, I was familiar with the body language that might indicate a potential cheater who decided to keep a closed-season game fish. The crappie and sunfish season was continuous all year, but it would be two weeks before the season for taking walleyes and northern pike would open and even longer for large-mouth bass.

As soon as the sun hit the treetops, two of the five boats drifted toward the access and loaded up. After they left, the remaining three continued to drift, occasionally boating a legal panfish. The darkness was beginning to obscure the details of the fishermen's actions, and soon it was too dim to identify anything other than the silhouetted outlines of the watercraft. I did notice one of the boats motor toward the access, stop for a moment, and then motor back toward the fishing area. I thought this a bit odd but passed it off at the time.

The red and green bow lights were the most visible items now that the sun had completely set. I decided to crawl closer to the access to observe the first of the three boats coming ashore and loading up on its trailer. I could check this outfit . . . or I could wait. Something made me wait! I don't know if it was the slightly peculiar action of the last boat or if it was just plain instinct, but I let it go. Another 15 minutes elapsed before the first boat made another pass by the access. I was preparing for its landing when it again veered back in the direction of the other boat. I could see little at that distance but assumed they were continuing to fish. Within ten minutes, the second boat pulled anchor and meandered toward the access into view of my binoculars. There were three young men, two of whom stayed with the boat while the other walked over the hill to fetch their car and trailer. "I could check these boys now," I pondered, "or I could be patient and only check the last boat, the one that approached the access twice earlier." It was a difficult decision. I wanted to check these guys in the worst way, but doing so would most likely expose my presence. I went with my gut instincts again; I waited and hung around in the dark!

Finally, just after the trailer lights disappeared over the hill, the final boat motored toward shore. This was the enjoyable part of the job—the reality of the moment pitted against your own instincts. They could be perfectly legal, which most people are, and I assumed would be the case. Or, they would be two fish perpetrators who had thought the coast was clear.

As they hit the shore, I decided to let them load up before making my approach out of the dark bushes. I thought it would be a lot easier to check their live-well when the boat was on the trailer and everyone was ready to leave than to jump in an unstable boat while everyone wandered around. "Hi, fellas, game warden. Like to check your catch," I pronounced as I walked up behind their trailer. "How's the fishing tonight?"

"We caught some sunfish," one of them blurted. "Otherwise, pretty slow." There was no reason for me to think any differently. They all seemed pretty calm and unthreatened by my sudden appearance.

"Might as well see what you have," I declared. "Why don't you jump up there and open your live-well." It didn't take long to notice that there was something amiss. None of them would take the initiative. "I guess I can do it myself," I said as I climbed aboard and searched for the compartment with my flashlight. "Ah, there it is. What do you have here?" As I surveyed the dark water, I could distinguish the backs of at least five species of fish. I reached into the cold recesses, coming up with two larger fish that were clinging to the bottom. By the myriad of species I observed, it was clear that they had kept everything they had caught. The well was loaded with largemouth bass, walleyes, northern pike and even some legal fish—crappies, sunfish and rock bass. These guys were nonspecific fish poachers. "Opening the season a little early, I see. What were you thinking?"

"The fish were biting good. Got a couple friends from out of state, so I thought, 'What the heck. Let's just go for it.' Anyway, we didn't think you'd be here."

That last statement was a real compliment. I was more often fooled by this type of folk than they were fooled by me. It felt good for a change to be able to say to myself on the way home that night, "You stuck to your instincts and it paid off."

EIGHT

The Swan Song

"Yes, the tundra swan does indeed sing a beautiful and haunting death song. In 1898, Daniel G. Elliot wrote of having been with a hunting party when a member of his group shot and mortally wounded a swan flying overhead. The swan set its wings and, Elliot wrote, 'sailing slowly down, began its death song, continuing it until it reached the water nearly half a mile away.' The song was not like any other swan note he had ever heard. Elliot inquired among local hunters and found that they too had heard that sad and beautiful song as a dying swan fell through the air. In 1955, H. A. Hochbaum wrote that, 'the departure song that is sung before they take off into the air is probably the swan song of legend, for when a swan is shot and falls crippled to the water, it utters this call as it tries in vain to rejoin its fellows in the sky.'" (*Reader's Digest Book of North American Birds*)

Game and fish enforcement work is inherently wrought with circumstances involving behavior that strongly suggests deficiencies in cerebral development. These occurrences have left me with a fervent desire to learn more about the reasoning behind some individuals' rotten judgments while afield. "Why would somebody do something like that?" is a question frequently posed to game wardens after hearing of some senseless incident—like discharging a load of bird-shot at a bear while grouse hunting or shooting a 25-five pound cub bear in your downtown yard. I could continue to add to this list of witnessed idiocy—pot-shooting a loon with a .22 rifle from a public access, (a $50.00 fine assessed on the shooter by a local judge), or dropping a 1-month-old fawn deer with buckshot in a residential driveway, sign shooting, and on and on! Add to this the fact that these types of violations are seldom ever solved—the perpetrators shamelessly thumbing their noses at the rules of ethics and sportsmanship.

Neither are these incidents limited to one age group, suggesting that the common denominator in most of this behavior is lack of education. Young kids who sit through a few hours of hunter safety classes and take to the field at 14 had better pick good friends. The young person's attitude toward ethical handling of a firearm can go either way according to the philosophy of his counterparts; the stage is set early. This is one reason some older folks are caught doing such juvenile things; they picked the wrong partners.

What would persuade four young people to cut the wire-mesh fencing surrounding a State research deer enclosure in Grand Rapids, knife two large bucks to death, and register them as legally taken deer? (The setback in accumulated research was immeasurable.) How does one really explain why a group of deer poachers would want to display the heads and hides of seven illegally taken antlerless deer along a county road and then call the warden to come and inspect what they had done? (See back cover.) How does one explain the purposeful snaring of three timber wolves and leaving their carcasses in the woods? Why have 80 percent of the bald eagles turned in to me throughout my career been found shot? (See back cover.) This behavior, of course, isn't restricted to hunting. How about the person or persons who stuffed a game warden's mailbox with the remains of freshly filleted before-season walleyes? Or shooting fish in the spring creeks with a shotgun?

I've declared all along that these are isolated incidents perpetrated by a few folks who have no clue of what hunting (or fishing) is all about, but what a damaging impact they can have, not just on the resource but on the whole sportsman image and the survival of our hunting traditions. We always have to keep in mind that only 20 percent of the American public hunts, so it becomes more important that we responsibly act as a group. "We good guys" have to rebuke the bad behavior out there. This means taking notes, staying aware . . . and reporting!

"Trumpeter swans had all but vanished by 1912, when the ornithologist Edward Howe Furbush wrote sadly, 'The trumpetings that were once heard over the breadth of a great continent will soon be heard no more.'

Luckily, just as the species seemed lost, with fewer than a hundred trumpeters known to exist, a national conservation policy was beginning to emerge. Now, there are several thousand throughout North America, their deep, resonant calls trumpeting a major conservation victory." (*Reader's Digest Book of North American Birds*)

It was only a few hours into a calm and mild opening morning of duck season when I heard a couple of my fellow officers chatting over the radio about an incident that had just occurred on a waterfowl lake south of Grand Rapids. Although sketchy, the information they had just received from a hunter had to do with a shot swan. Apparently this individual had seen a trumpeter swan, the larger of the two swans species found in Minnesota, fall from the air following a barrage of shots coming from the opposite side of the lake.

After meeting with the two officers, we studied the information at hand and decided on a two-pronged approach. One officer would interview the witness to attempt to get a hint about the shooter's identity. Hopefully, this would also eliminate the informant as a possible suspect and more easily direct our investigation to someone else on the lake. The other two officers would use a boat in an attempt to find the big white bird. It was important that we knew for sure there *was* an attempted shooting before further energy was expended.

I elected to look for the swan. Other hunters had already left the lake, so interviewing any other possible witnesses was out of the question. Finding the evidence was an absolute necessity. Without it, the case would swiftly come to an end. The hunter also mentioned that he wasn't sure the swan was dead; he thought it a possibility it had just been wounded.

We pushed out onto the thousand acres of quiet water, started the 4-horse, and made our way to all the bays and recesses where a 30-pound feathered creature could hide. After an hour of scouring the bulrush and cattail shoreline, including the numerous floating bogs scattered about the lake, we felt our chances of ever making a case shrinking rapidly. "What do you think?" I inquired of my partner. "A waste of time or should we keep going?"

Let's go back and talk to the witness again and see if our partner found out anything more."

We were greeted by a bit of new information. Our tipster had also recorded three separate license plate numbers from vehicles parked at the access. The lot was empty now, but the numbers could certainly be a help. "Let's run them and find out if any come back to a local resident or cabin owner. We could make a few visits before dark," I suggested.

We discovered that two of the plate numbers belonged to folks who were impossible to check out that day because of the distance they lived from the lake. One, however, came back "not on file." This either meant a new car not yet placed on the records or our witness was a number off on the ID; a three could have been mistaken for an eight or some similar slip-up. We decided to have the State Patrol run the probable options through their computer to see if anyone with local connections might pop up. "Found one here with an address from that area," the dispatcher stated within 15 minutes. "First number may have been written down incorrectly. Maybe worth checking out." And we did!

My partners headed for the residence about 10 miles away while I stayed with the equipment at the access and discussed the situation with the caller. I was hoping for something positive, an inkling of evidence that might somehow connect a shooter to the bird. After further discussion with the witness, it was unmis-takable that the event had occurred. He was a rock-solid and totally credible individual who seemed to be as disturbed as us about the shooting and as concerned in catching the culprit. "You know," I said glumly, "these folks are rarely, if ever caught." I didn't mean to put a lid on our hopes, but I could count on one hand how many of these indiscriminate shooting cases had been successfully investigated.

Within an hour, my two partners drove up. "I don't think we have much," they stated, a bit dejected. "He may be our man, but without the swan as evidence, we're at a loss. He completely denied any knowledge of a shot swan. He admitted to being on the lake, but saw nothing."

"That's a little strange. It was hard, when the flock of giant birds flew down the lake, and 'boom,' one fell from the sky, not to notice," replied our witness.

"We'll try to do some follow-up," I said. "Give us your num-ber so we can keep in touch."

Two days later, I got a call from our DNR pilot that he had spotted what appeared to be a large white bird on the same lake. Accompanied by a fellow officer and a wildlife employee, we arrived on the scene, canoe in tow. Through the bog, two of us paddled out from the north shore. Resting in the tall grass about a mile down the shore was our big bird—apparently still alive. It must have been much more lively two days earlier, allowing it to hide from sight. As we approached, we could see that one of the wings had been badly injured. Carefully urging the bird into the canoe, we sadly realized we were dealing with a creature in grave condition. The great bird was almost dead, its right wing now infected and its energy spent.

Arriving back at our vehicle, we let our wildlife expert make the decision as to the swan's fate. "It's too far gone to send to the raptor center," he stated. "It's been too long. It should be put out of its misery without delay." With that, we placed the carcass in the box of our truck and headed back. We now had the evi-dence, but what to do with it was the big question.

Illegally shot 30-pound trumpeter swan found alive. It did not survive.

It seemed like the end of the story. The weeks flew by as ice now covered most of the shallow lakes. The waning days of the 60-day waterfowl season drew scaup and other diving ducks into the larger waters, and winter was only two weeks away.

A phone call from Officer Dennis on a wintry Saturday morning suddenly renewed my memory of the swan episode. "I've been mulling over that swan case, Tom. Remember when the guy we interviewed said he knew nothing about the shooting? Something's not right. It makes less and less sense to me the more I think about it. Whatdaya say we make another visit to his cabin tonight? We'll just take a chance he's up for the weekend. One last interview won't hurt!"

We met about 7:00 p.m. at the end of the quarter-mile driveway. It was snowing heavily, the huge flakes that fall when the temperature is just below freezing, and it was dark, the moon just entering its new-moon phase. As we walked down the curved path, I couldn't help think that even a first-class mystery novel couldn't conjure up the mood we felt from the scene of ghostly surroundings, the narrow brush-lined trail, the snow and the complete silence.

As we stepped around the final barrier of trees, there it was—a small cabin with a yellowish light emanating from the kitchen window . . . he was there! "Game wardens," we both announced after the door partially opened in response to our two knocks. "I know it's late, but would you mind if we chatted with you a minute . . . about that swan that was shot a couple of months ago? I know we talked to you already, but we have a few more questions. Mind if we come in?"

I tried to study his reaction the best I could in the dim light when our suspect first spied our uniforms. There is never a guarantee on a prediction of guilt, but I was pretty convinced that our trip might be worthwhile. We declined an invitation to sit and started right in about our intent. We wanted to know why he hadn't seen a flock of swans or heard from anybody at the access that day about a large swan being shot. "I don't know anything about a swan," he kept repeating. "I'm the past president of the local chapter of Ducks Unlimited back in my home town. I wouldn't do anything like this. I've been hunting that lake for years."

"Now we have another powerful motive for denial," I thought. Embarrassment and humiliation—some of the most powerful emotions to deter people from committing wildlife crimes. We've got to push this guy a little further. "You can tell us to leave anytime you feel like it, sir," I kept repeating. "You have no obligation to talk to us. We just want to get to the bottom of this, and we think you're the man. Now it's out on the table."

His continual denials and profuse sweating told my partner and I to notch it up one more step. We elected to try the "good guy-bad guy" method of interrogation, a scheme as old as the hills but still effective under certain conditions. Maybe these were those conditions! "You know, sir, my buddy has a little problem with a short fuse, if you know what I mean. His patience is running thin, and I'm not sure I can restrain him after a certain point. I'm saying to you, he's getting upset about your lying. (Notice I'm the good guy.) Why don't you and I go sit down over there and you tell me the whole story. I promise I won't interrupt you. I guarantee you'll feel better. We'll all feel better, and you can get this great big burden off your chest. We're only talking misdemeanor here! A summons and we're out of here."

We didn't make it to the couch. The tears came before the "I did it." The suspect completely broke down and surrendered himself to our compassion. After one hour of pent-up emotion and denial, he was set free. Our strung-out perpetrator began to "sing." "It was foggy. I shot at what I thought was a white goose. The minute I pulled the trigger, I knew something was wrong. I saw it soar down the lake, so I just got out of there."

"There, that wasn't so bad," I said in a genuinely sympathetic tone. "The only thing I want to say is, if you would have admitted it that first day, we might have been able to save the bird. You know what I mean?"

"Sorry! There's a lot of things I SHOULD have done, but I didn't and I regret that. I certainly should have known better."

The $3,500 fine that was assessed and a one-year license revocation was as strong a penalty, other than a jail sentence, that could be assessed at the time. I didn't think the penalty was as important as the lessons that this individual learned and hopefully passed on to others.

I'm convinced he had no intention of shooting a rare trumpeter swan. (There are only 200 nesting pair in the entire state.) I'm sure he made a mistake, but as I said in the beginning, a senseless act is always preceded by a dumb decision. His was to shoot something before completely identifying, a must-do for waterfowl hunting. I've never completely come to terms with exactly who should be held responsible in these types of cases. Every situation is different. I realize intent is important. "But if the guy didn't have intent . . . " I always heard.

Isn't there a certain amount of responsibility to identify your prey and become educated in the sport to which you are about to devote lots of time and money? It certainly would reduce these "mistakes."

By the way, kudos to the informant and his good judgment. These are the folks that help guarantee a fair playing field out there in our marshes, woods and waters.

NINE

The Search For Trout

Discovering large over-limits of fish is a very difficult job for enforcement personnel; in fact, the number of cases made every year are relatively small in comparison to the sum total of all types of fishing infractions. This does not suggest that there aren't significant numbers of fish being possessed and transported illegally, but it does mean that folks who intend to violate the fishing rules can do so with little fear of being exposed.

The rules by which all peace officers are bound do not allow, and rightly so, the indiscriminate searching of homes, vehicles, cabins or other buildings or locations, where a person has a reasonable expectation of privacy. "Probable cause" to search these private places is compulsory for all law enforcement in this country—just check out the Fourth Amendment of the Constitution—game wardens being no exception.

The three basic means by which an officer can legally search vehicles and property are the detection of probable cause for an immediate search, the possession of a search warrant based on probable cause, and consent. In addition, there are many other restrictions that may be specific to each case and of which an officer must be aware before executing a search.

Although recreational vehicles like boats are less bound by the rules of search (a game warden can check live-wells, coolers and compartments where fish could be stored as well as hunters' game bags), a dark house or fish shelter may not be entered without permission.

All these restrictions to guarantee the public's right to privacy provide the motivation for game wardens to make great efforts to obtain direct evidence—that is, when a violation is witnessed in full view of the officer. The majority of arrests by game wardens are made this way. However, many of the bigger over-limit fish and wildlife cases are prosecuted due to an accumulation of circumstantial evidence which eventually leads to the implementation of a search warrant. Following are two cases in point.

Like many of the bigger cases, this one started with a call from a concerned citizen. Most calls from the public provide us with bits and pieces of information and must be enhanced and investigated before enforcement action can be taken, particularly if the witness is unwilling to testify as to what he or she saw.

He was providing only enough clues to "steer" me toward an individual whom he had suspected of accumulating walleyes. I knew the informer as a resort owner with a somewhat shaky past, but this didn't deter me from expending some hours investigating this complaint, especially when the person in question was a nonresident who was fishing a very productive lake.

My first act was to approach the area in question and monitor the person's movements. This involved hiding my vehicle and making a couple of "walk-throughs" around the property while attempting to identify the boat, the motor home and the individual himself. All this prework would contribute to the mound of evidence I would eventually need to obtain a search warrant, if it ever came to that. My chief aim was to become familiar with the person and his fishing behavior—how often did he fish, what time of the day, where did he clean the fish and was anyone else involved? I also chatted on a regular basis with the informant in order to elicit more assistance since he was able, but not always willing, to keep an eye on the person every day. These get-togethers bettered our relationship, and in time, proved essential to the case.

My choices on how to proceed came down to two: I would have to watch the person fish, and I would have to keep track of the fish remains in the fish-cleaning shelter. The latter was simpler than observing his fishing activity. Surveillance of a fisherman, particularly one who is violating the law, is difficult at best. Struggling to avoid detection, and my attempts to position myself properly—every day—was a time-consuming affair.

At mid-morning on the third day, I figured he had caught and kept over three limits of walleyes. This was verified by inspection of the "gut bucket" that evening. Doing the math and allowing for another person in his party, he had already violated the limit laws and appeared now, to be "stocking up."

Convinced that my time investment was worthwhile, I chose to continue my close watch and gather more evidence that would, in due course, prompt me to draft a search warrant on the man's 20-foot motor home.

My fish-hog suspect continued his wayward conduct the next two days. Recognizing that he was booked for two weeks and tomorrow would be his sixth day, I made the decision to hit the courthouse the next morning and apply for a "looking paper." I felt that data collected the last five days would be more than sufficient to support the probable cause prerequisite for obtaining a search warrant.

On the afternoon of the sixth day, my partner Ken and I arrived at the resort with a signed search warrant for the trailer and specific surrounding property. Our knock at the door was met by a gentleman of late middle age who was taken aback by our appearance and subsequent search request. "Yeah, I have a few fish in the freezer, but I think I'm OK. My wife is here with me."

"Then you sure won't mind if we take a look. We want you to know that we do have a search warrant which also includes your vehicle and boat."

"Go ahead. Only freezer we have is the top of the refrigerator."

As soon as Ken and I peered in the freezer, our gut feelings about this guy proved out. The entire freezer section was chock-full with packages of fillets, each neatly wrapped in aluminum foil. Further search of the boat and vehicle uncovered nothing of interest.

Then it was time to count the individual fillets in the broiling July heat. With a temperature of 90 degrees inside, the tally continued to rise. Soon it was clear that a major over-limit of fish was about to be uncovered—50, 60, 70, and finally, 87 walleyes—174 fillets were lying on the kitchen table. Our prior intelligence also pointed out that our fish poacher had given fish to neighboring tenants. All these fish and he still had eight more days of vacation! We theorized what the final damage to the resource would have been by then.

It took a little time for our defendant to calm down and begin opening up about his past. He certainly was his own person and expressed this with great stories of his younger days, including submarine assignments during World War II. Our drive to the bank to post bail was pleasant enough. His remark on why he didn't buy his wife a fishing license: "I didn't want to spend the money!"

This next case began on a beautiful fall day in September. My day's patrol took me past a designated trout lake about 20 miles north of Grand Rapids in the Chippewa National Forest.

The fishing pressure is seldom heavy on this small undeveloped lake, allowing for a quick and easy inspection from the bordering state highway. "No one on the lake today," I reflected as the massive white pines passed by my creeping truck. "Except that car again!"

This was the third time in as many days that I had spotted this same sedan parked on a small path 30 feet above the water's edge. I thought, rather than check a license right away, I would watch the fisherman for a time from a distance.

As I crouched in some brush, I scrutinized the older gentleman's fishing action. As he put a fourth rainbow trout on a stringer, it appeared he had only one fish to go for his legal limit of five. Soon after the next re-baiting of a night crawler, a fifth and final fish was jerked from the quiet waters and added to the stringer. As he climbed the hill back to his vehicle, I made a decision to again pass up a license check. I became curious about this guy's repeated trips and wondered if he would return for another limit. I concluded that continued monitoring in this case should take precedence over a trout stamp check.

The following morning I returned to the same place, same time and observed the same vehicle parked in the usual location. "Interesting. Day four, and most likely a limit every time," I pondered. As I watched for a second time, it appeared be the same scenario—a limit of fish in a relatively short period. Now I began to question how many times a day he was showing up.

After cleaning up other obligations, I elected to spend more time observing and tracking the next day. The routine was the same: catch five trout and leave. But this time, I ate my lunch and waited. This little move proved worthwhile. My proficient trout fisherman returned. That said it all . . . he was "double-tripping!" And yet another limit of trout bore that out.

Now I had a case, but the question was, how long was this going to continue and where was he keeping his cache? I would have to follow him!

The Illinois license plate confirmed that he was a part-time visitor to the area, maybe a cabin owner or resort client. As I tagged along at a safe distance, our journey ended at a long driveway on the west side of a lake about ten miles south. I had guessed correctly; he was a seasonal cabin owner.

Over the next week, I attempted to inspect the fishing site daily. The same car was parked in the same spot every day all week. It was now time to rise to the next step. A search warrant was my only chance simultaneously to retrieve the poached fish and arrest the individual. My job was to convince the county attorney and judge that my week of observations constituted a reasonable belief that an over-limit of trout was being possessed. I would have to put up a pretty good argument that it was unreasonable to think this guy ate all the fish he caught. I had to demonstrate, by showing cases similar to this from the past, that he was an accumulator and would most likely be leaving the state with a trunk full of very valuable fish. By valuable, I mean, the State estimates each trout planted in a designated trout lake (a lake that has been modified to hold only trout species) costs about $6.00 per fish. The special trout stamp required to fish in these waters helps defray these costs.

A good friend had helped by keeping an eye on the residence in question. He lived closer and was able to make routine inspections of any changes at the cabin, including signs of packing up. He also had that "civilian" look and was able to approach the man without suspicion.

And that is, in fact, what he did the following morning. As he made a pass by the driveway, he noticed that the mailbox was missing and had apparently been "taken in" for the season. He decided to enter the driveway and approach the resident as a person "looking for an address." That visit yielded the most helpful information. He was leaving today . . . back to Illinois.

As soon as the call was received, I shifted into high gear. Down to the County Attorney's office I ran, carrying all the evidence that I had amassed.

"Appears you might have a pretty good case here, Tom," said the judge as he signed the warrant. "Good luck"

In the meantime, I called my neighboring officer, Willy, for assistance. Internal rules stated that we would never execute a search warrant alone.

As we made our way up the gravel driveway, we spotted the same large sedan facing our direction with the trunk open. Behind the rear bumper was our suspect stooped over the trunk, apparently loading items for his imminent trip south. We were both out of our vehicle and only feet away before he recognized our uniforms. "Sir, we have reason to believe that you may have a stockpile of trout on your premises, and we are presenting you with this search warrant to look in your freezers," I explained, as I handed him a copy of the form. Other than a person exercising on a hot day, I've never seen an individual who was sweating as profusely as this individual. A rather large man, he was breathing so deeply and dripping water in such quantity that I was immediately concerned about his health. "We're just here to take a look, sir. Could you guide us to the location of your refrigerator or freezer?"

"Sure, just got the one in the house. Follow me."

At the same time, Willy was inspecting the newly built garage and hollered from its locked door, "What's in here? Sounds like a motor running. Is that a freezer?"

A quick denial finally surrendered to a, "Yeah, I'll open it for ya."

We looked into a garage empty other than for a freezer standing directly to our right. Opening the freezer revealed everything that I had suspected. Each compartment was crammed full of packaged whole trout, their red lateral stripes still visible through the plastic bags.

A further inspection of the cabin freezer revealed more trout in the same condition, cleaned and frozen. His wife met us and assisted with the check, further revealing that she had never purchased a fishing license. My thought on this: "Why are these types of poachers so cheap, that seldom do the accompanying spouses ever have a license to at least cover a second limit?" This has been a recurring scenario over the years.

As we did a full inventory and issued a misdemeanor summons, he revealed that he had been planning on leaving within ten minutes of our arrival. The only thing he had left to do was to pack two coolers with fish that would fit perfectly into the trunk space he was preparing as we drove up. This was a close one! Just a few more minutes and they would have been history. I have little doubt that these fish were packaged for resale...total count, 95 rainbow trout! Making a profit from our fish only compounds the sin.

A final note: This was the second trip he had taken to his cabin that summer, and he had owned the cabin more than 15 years. Do the math!

Ninety-two rainbow trout discovered in freezer minutes before the violator was to leave the state.

TEN

The Fearless Lady

In my first book, *Poachers Caught*, the final sentences of Chapter Three read: "*Two years later, my little lady's husband went out to his pasture on an autumn night after hearing shots fired on his property. He never returned! Three weeks of searching with dogs, planes and numerous search teams were unsuccessful. It has been twenty years. You decide!*" That was an incomplete account of an incident that I have agonized over for years. After much personal deliberation and soul searching, I've decided to disclose additional pieces of this intriguing and painful puzzle. As before, readers will have to decide for themselves!

This is a story with many players, all of whom will **not** be identified in the following chronicles. It's unfortunate that many of these people who could possibly add credence to the events are no longer with us. Also, this is not an investigation of any potential wrongdoing; it is merely an attempt on my part to offer an alternative version of what may have taken place.

Poaching in central Itasca County was widespread during my tenure as a game warden. I don't just flippantly throw those words out—I experienced it! Many of my encounters were revealed in my first book. Now I would like to divulge my 15-year relationship with one person who totally committed herself to battling the poaching element on and around her homestead. Yes, this is the woman, now deceased, whose missing husband has never been found. A spirited lady to say the least, she became my informant and guide for most of my enforcement efforts in that area. For sure, her courage and relentless desire to help subdue the local poaching element will never be underestimated or forgotten by me. If I ever had a mentor for strength and integrity, it was she. I remember her first call very well. It was 1976 and a strong voice suggested that I make a trip to her residence–the 20-mile trip would not be in vain. "Please park behind the barn," she remarked. "I don't want them to see your car."

I assumed "them" meant the local poachers. As I walked to her door, I was greeted by an older woman, who, although only 5 feet tall, exuded a confident and self-assured presence.

"My husband's out doing chores," she said. "C'mon in. I want to tell you some things."

This was the start of a long and captivating relationship that repeatedly left me dumbfounded. I would have a hard time in the next 15 years living up to her expectations. What I would hear that first warm fall afternoon not only changed many of the enforcement tactics and methods that I had employed up until then, but it also instilled in me a sense of just how dangerous this job could be.

"I doubt if you are aware of the true magnitude of the poaching that goes on around here," she stated with an unwavering stare. "There's some real problems around here, and they started generations ago." As she proceeded to inform me of the "families" and "poaching gangs," I could only think of the trust she had to have in me to reveal these very secretive activities and of how she was putting herself in jeopardy if certain folks discovered her eagerness to provide specifics. The method by which she accumulated this information will never be revealed, but I knew after the first five minutes, she was for real. I left her home with a renewed desire to dig right in. I would start that evening, mapping and planning strategy for future excursions. I also became more cautious!

Within months, her phone calls almost ceased. She said it was not safe to continue to use the party line as everyone listened to each other's conversations up there. From then on, she mostly communicated by letters. And write she did. Many times I would receive two, three-page, handwritten notes in a month. (I received over 40 letters during those years, of which there are only 18 remaining.) I now share some of her thoughts and the circumstances surrounding her and her husband's valiant struggle in waging war with the local poachers. Remember, these are direct passages from her personal correspondence. Names and non-pertinent details have been purposely omitted as indicated.

September 26, 1976

Since you were here yesterday, I got to thinking this night how I could help you (. . . .) I don't like to call on telephone. We are on party line with all these people. (. . . .) I am also including a list of names that you might check to see if they buy licenses. (. . . .) You asked me where the old road goes in back of our place . . . that is a wild area with sloughs, pugholes, small lakes and birch hills. Wonderful hunting area for ducks.

October 12, 1976

Now there's been a lot of shooting around here for years, and I always gave them the benefit of the doubt. But last Friday night they came in here about 7:00 p.m. in evening. It was right here on our field. Mrs. __said she had tried to call me that they were coming but she couldn't get me. The reason she is talking I guess is her relatives just want her to die so they can sell her place. (. . . .) I hope you keep right after those . . . til you get them good. Looks like they want the whole country. Saturday there was a jeep went down that road. If my husband had told me sooner, I would have taken a chance and called. ____ has a jeep in his yard!

November 8, 1976

Congratulations! I see you got some of the buzzards. ____ says they have been at it all summer. We were served venison, so I guess they get it all right. (. . . .) Well if they do as they usually do there is going to be a lot of hunting going on before hunting season opens up. ____ know they are hard to catch in the brush, but catch that bunch of buzzards, just like damn mafia.

March 15, 1977

Our dog is definitely gone. He was here at 7:00 a.m. The dog did not chase cars and would only run as far as the mailbox. Whoever done away with the dog must have laid for him there in the gravel pit; and then hauled him off so there would be no chance to examine him (. . . .) I am not blaming you for anything. I sure can see the difficult job you have got, but that bunch is so rotten. I blame ____! This is pure spite. These old pros do their hunting in daylight hours. Early morning or evening. They mostly hunt on their days off because they all work shifts. (. . . .) I am going to watch that road back there. I am also going to mark the road so I know when a car has gone down there during the night. I sure want you to know that I think you are OK and I want you to win. I am 100% on your side. You better watch those s.o.b.'s. Take a partner along. I know they are mean.

April 11, 1977

Some kids found our dog down on the lakeshore. He had a bullet right through his rib cage (. . . .) I guess he got even! Well, I intend to get a little even too. I am watching the road close anytime after the 4th of July they start. In past you hear the shooting early in the evening. I suppose anytime after daybreak too; but I am sleeping then. I don't think they headlight on our field because I am a poor sleeper and I think I would hear the shooting in fact I know I would. They headlight the place next ____ for years. When I call and tell you I hear shooting across the swamp, I mean all that creek area and that field. If it is ____ they will bring the deer up behind ____ barn or go across the old road where ____ place is. Another place is ____'s place, probably during daylight hours with plenty of traffic on the road. (. . . .) If I call and tell you the shooting is back of our buildings, I will mean somewhere along that old road you found. They may bring the deer out at ____'s place. Don't overlook that area back of Hanson Lake. (. . . .) Maybe they will switch their operations there. Start early, just as early as you think deer are good eating and before. I think right after the 4th of July. All August and September they sure go to it. Well, you understand better what you are up against and good luck at all the buzzards. I think you are going to have better luck. If they were just occasional offenders, it wouldn't be bad but they are really something. Good luck.

June 8, 1977

My husband found a tree in swamp where they had made a ladder way up. They cut brush and trees around this tree so they could look out on fields, so I guess this is how they knew the deer were feeding on field. (. . . .) Watch those ___ kids. They are too dumb and cocky to be careful. And that oldest one, he is dumb enough to shoot you. (. . . .) They are going to start early. They can't wait. We have had a few deer around.

August 8, 1977

Now when you are back of our place here on that old road, you will see a road the Minn. P&L put in. (. . . .) That area always had moose in there, but you know how long they last with these guys around here. You should become familiar with the area. (. . . .) If you can't understand my directions, I'll take you over and show you. There is plenty of shooting goes on a couple days before hunting season back there around those little pughole lakes.

August 23, 1977

Another guy to watch ___! He lived somewhere around Minneapolis before moving here (. . . .) He always came up every year to hunt with these guys so I suppose he moved up here to hunt the year around.

Oct 13, 1977

___ was over and told me that each of the culprits was fined $750. Tom, when you got ___ you got one half the mafia. I hope you got a good look at the other one. You got them in their stomping grounds. My neighbor came in the door, "they got the big shot," laughing all over herself. She said, "Those boys have been on your place many times (. . . .) They got away with lots of deer. I don't think they'll quit. The fine won't hurt them." (. . . .) My husband took a walk for himself. Behind our buildings there is an old road that goes back to ___! He was amazed to see how they had opened up that road, but he said you couldn't get through with any jeep now, too much water. He walked all the way around and said he didn't see any deer tracks on road until he got close to our field. (. . . .) So if you have men and could listen here on field you might get somebody. They will come in back of pasture or make a stand on the road back there. Most likely late afternoon. Somebody owes you and your wife a night out on the town for getting old ___!

October 31, 1977

My husband says he can show you the illegal stands behind our build-ings. Somebody crippled a deer about 11:30 p.m. Saturday night on ___'s field. They don't know who it was but they heard the shots. I saw two men in hunting clothes and boat and guns. They have just moved in the neighborhood and go out long before season and shoot off partridge. I sup-pose you have to be in forty places at once. If I hear shooting late at night on our field. You keep in mind about that guy across from ___'s house.

June 16, 1978

(. . . .) When you go west past ___'s place, there is a good sized piece of plowed. On the east end of this plowing there is a little road goes back (. . . .) There is sure to be head lighters on this area, I'll bet.

October 20, 1979

I guess you couldn't help but hear about the trouble we had here. (She's referring to her missing husband.) *Did the deputies tell you about the remains of deer found west of us? So they are still out. You can bet that is ___'s and ___'s. (. . . .) Some of the local women stayed with me and one said that the whole gang went down the river in boat and shooting bear. Said they got fourteen bear and had papers on all of them. So if they take fourteen bear, how many deer do they take? (. . . .) Lay out in brush from five o clock in evening back on that old road. They are too smart to headlight. The wardens who get that mob should get a paid vacation in Las Vegas. Watch out for them. They are mean and ___ would be the worst one if cornered. The whole bunch are mean.*

June 13, 1980

Two of your poachers living on the lake, according to the neighbors, were shooting ducks early in the morning this spring. (. . . .) There are no deer left around here. I may have four or five but they are sure disappearing.

July 14, 1983

I seem to have quite a few deer around here this year. The fellow put-ting up the hay says there are a lot of beds down near the swamp. (. . . .) I am feeding them salt here in my barnyard to try to keep them close to the house. I saw a big doe. She was a whopper, the kind that should produce three young. She was pretty. I suppose it is about time they will start their hunting. It will be daylight hours, late afternoon. ___ and ___ will come in from the north. If you are out this way around ten in the evening, I will show you how to drive up behind the buildings without being detected, even if I had visitors (. . . .) I suppose you got a good flashlight so I can show you where to go.

1984 - 1989 Lost correspondence.

Nov 29,1990 *You won't have to worry about ___ anymore. I am sending you a clipping of his death. (. . . .) No hunters on my field this year. Wish you Happy Christmas.* (final correspondence)

What you decide to glean from these odds and ends is up to you. I still continue to pose the question: What happened to my informant's husband?

ELEVEN

The Kitchen Capers

One of the reasons the job of a game warden can be so intriguing and captivating is the freedom that the officer enjoys to pursue cases that could not otherwise be solved with general patrolling or the use of standard investigation techniques. An officer's menu of tactics and schemes are only limited by his imagination. As long as the rules of search and seizure are adhered to and department policies are followed, many unusual strategies can be employed to catch those game and fish violators who would most likely never be apprehended.

Catching folks selling fish was always one of the more difficult violations to uncover. Selling or bartering game fish is against the law. Commercializing on our public resource is considered by most sportsmen to be a serious offense, and for good reason . . . we would soon have few fish left if a dollar bill was attached to each walleye.

The rumors of fish sales abounded in Itasca County, but attaining enough information to make an arrest was darn near impossible. The folks involved were very secretive in their methods of distribution, resulting in minimal enforcement contacts over the years. The only options were to covertly establish rapport with the potential violators or to befriend persons who were in businesses where larger transactions might take place. I chose the latter.

It didn't take long to learn that fresh walleyes were being sold in large quantities to various restaurants in the community. These fish were shipped into town from several locations including Rainy Lake and both the Leech Lake and Red Lake Indian Reservations.

Rumors were that fillets from freshly netted walleyes were being traded in quantities ranging from three or four fish being sold to one individual up to hundreds, even thousands of fish, being wholesaled to commercial establishments all over the area. The netting and sale of such large quantities of illegal fish were in large part the cause of the limit reductions and eventual end to fishing on some of the producing lakes.

The first place I concentrated my efforts was a popular restaurant in the heart of Grand Rapids. The owner at that time was a person with whom I had made friends and had come to trust. During our various jaunts into the hinterlands while accompanying me as a civilian ride-along, he would mention how he would occasionally be approached by "locals" wanting to sell him fresh walleye fillets. In time, I gained the courage to float a proposal by him involving a possible set-up at his establishment. I had no idea how he would react, but I also knew that this was one of those rare opportunities. I had to make a bust and send a message to those folks profiting from our public resources.

"You bet I would," he said without hesitation. "I don't believe in any of this illegal stuff going on. What do you want to do?" I was a bit surprised by his straightforwardness due to the fact that he knew he was putting himself on the line, which was unusual for a civilian. I knew I was partnering with a good man!

My job now was to coordinate some sort of a "sting" that would lure a culprit into a setting where he would be caught red-handed with the goods. Not only did I want the individual apprehended with an illegal possession of fish but also I needed the actual transaction to be witnessed by other officers to show intent of sale and hopefully guarantee an open-and-shut case. I asked my partner to call me the next time he was contacted by a potential seller and that I would get things rolling.

It didn't take long. Within a week, he had filled me in on an individual who was willing to deliver as many fish as he needed. I suggested that he arrange a date and time for the drop and update me on the specifics once the final arrangements were made. I immediately called my Special Investigative Unit backup team to assist with the essentials for a setup.

Our strategy was to place a couple undercover officers in the kitchen proper, both dressed as cooks. The two-man backup team would be outside awaiting a radio signal that the deal had gone down. The delivery would take place through the back

Numerous packages containing 550 walleyes illegally sold to a local restaurant.

door at 1:00 a.m. As half of the backup team, I felt this arrangement was more than adequate to protect the establishment's clients as well as securing the offender with the least disturbance. I always thought one could never be too careful in any situation involving a money transaction.

As we prepared for the evening's work, I couldn't help feeling we might actually be able to pull this thing off. Not that I'm a pessimist, but I can count on one hand the cases like this that went down exactly as planned. The apprehension was building, much of it due to watching two officers dress up in their kitchen cook attire, including chef's hats and white aprons. Also, it's rare that the employees making up your BLT are carrying 9-mm handguns under their shirts.

The solitary, blond-haired driver in a dark sedan was right on time. As we watched him back up to the door, it was obvious that the trunk was weighted down. Its rear springs were bottomed out, forcing the car's headlights to shine at an upward angle. "If all that weight is fish, this is going to be big," I thought. "I hope the boys inside can bring this to a quick conclusion."

As the tall gentleman exited the car and proceeded through the back door, I got ready for the call. This would signal that the transaction had been made and the man was in custody. We intently watched as box after box was carried from the open trunk. As I waited I thought, "What a huge sacrifice my friend just made!" He had no idea what the consequences might be for his business or his reputation in the community. But here we were, waiting for one of the biggest sales ever of illegal fish, all because of this person's commitment to doing the right thing. It lifted my spirit!

"C'mon in, Tom. Everything's under control," the voice blared from my car radio. As I entered through the back door, I could see a large portion of the floor strewn with frost-covered plastic bags, each about the size of two softballs. My partners, still wearing the chef's hats, smiled as I walked up to the anxious defendant, now in handcuffs. I immediately recognized the individual as one of my long-suspected fish traffickers. Finally," I thought, "something went smoothly. We got him!"

A sense of relief was evident on the faces of all officers involved. But the vast amount of fish brought us quickly back to reality. There were more than 70 packages containing a total of 550 walleyes—1100 fillets! We also learned that this was only half the fish he was to sell that evening; it was just all that the trunk could handle in one load.

A hefty fine was handed down along with a small jail sentence. As I look back on this particular incident and consider the illegal profit that was being made at the expense of our resource, I wonder what impact it really had on the overall illicit marketing of fish in the area. When profits are so high, it probably only makes a dent.

This same location about ten years later was the scene of another incident involving fish. Perch fishing on Lake Winnibigoshish was in full swing when we followed some over-limit suspects into the parking lot of the restaurant. My partner and I hid across the street watching from our patrol unit while two uniformed wardens pulled into the lot and entered the establishment. Our plan was to see how our perpetrators reacted when they saw the game wardens.

Our little plan worked perfectly. The two occupants got out, did their casual "looking around" thing, and then grabbed two buckets of fish from the back of their pickup. One of them picked up both buckets and tiptoed down the line of vehicles, placing them both behind another pickup truck. We got the whole thing on film and let them go in to eat lunch before confronting them as they walked out of the restaurant. We were glad that the unsuspecting owner of the pickup hadn't come out, or he might have unknowingly backed over two buckets containing 140 perch.

My second commercial fish bust was analogous to the first. About a year later, I obtained information of more fish being sold at another well-known restaurant close to town. It also involved a good relationship I had fostered with the owner and his willingness to take part in a slightly more elaborate setup, one involving a video camera. My friend said he had been approached more than once to buy walleyes for his customers and had in fact done so in the past. He knew it was illegal and thought it was about time to come clean and help me with the apprehension of the suspects.

Knowing little about video recording at that time, I left it up to the owner to find the proper positioning and location for the camera and potential transaction. Our plan was to hide the camera in a ceiling corner of the shipping and receiving area where a wide-angle view of the suspects could be recorded. This was accomplished well in advance, and I just waited for the telephone call that would signal a delivery of fish. For insurance, we also gave my informant $500.00 worth of marked bills to be used in the sale.

The call came within two days. "Four people," he said. "They will be here about 1:00 p.m. I'll inform you as to the type and color of vehicle when they arrive. You take it from there."

After the call, I, along with a fellow officer, pulled up as close as we could get without being conspicuous. We found we were forced to remain in the main parking lot out front because of the lack of parking behind the building. This procedure didn't allow us to maintain continual surveillance of the blue sedan; we would have to stop them as they drove into view on their way to the highway.

It seemed like we had just gotten set up when we saw the rusty, four-door sedan skidding around the corner of the building and heading through the parking lot in the direction of the highway 600 feet away. The call from our informant confirming the deal came the same instant I shouted, "We've got to stop them before they get in the traffic." It was too late! Even though we were right on their tail, the old car shot out into the heavy, westbound traffic. After engaging our red lights and siren, I steered the patrol vehicle across two lanes of eastbound autos and began a pursuit with the commercial fish poachers.

I was quite sure they would pull over when they noticed our lit-up vehicle on their rear bumper. This was not the case, however, and our fish-peddling escapees were now dodging oncoming cars and trucks while passing everything ahead of them. As we entered the city limits, I called for a local PD car to assist me with the stop. "We'll block them off at Highways 2 and 169," a familiar voice shot back.

Less than a mile from that position, I could see all kinds of movement inside the vehicle. "Just watch for anything thrown out," I hollered at my partner while I tried to maintain control. Even though the speeds hadn't exceeded 50 miles per hour, it seemed like very little time had elapsed before I spotted police lights flashing in the distance.

The object of our pursuit pulled over to the curb right downtown, allowing us to park to their rear and approach them on foot. Two police officers had arrived at the same time and assisted in the removal of all four suspects. After informing each of his right to remain silent and applying handcuffs, we began searching for the marked money. First we searched each person, including socks, shoes, shirts, pants and wallets. Nothing! We then spent the next 15 minutes rummaging around the inside of the car. We checked everything that could remotely contain the bills: in the seats, under the seats, glove compartment, heater vents and dash areas, under the dash, under the steering wheel, ashtrays, even checking the roof fabric for slits. Nothing . . . not a sign of a bill!

"OK, boys," I explained. "If you won't produce the goods, you all have to make a trip to the jail while we impound your car for further inspection."

"Whatever you've got to do," one of them muttered. "We don't have nothing."

That afternoon, three of us started a more extensive search. After checking with the informant, we learned that $240.00 had been handed to them for the fish. The money had to be somewhere in their rust bucket.

We were into our third hour of searching—not a sign of a cent! It was time to get the tools out and start some interior stripping. I remained totally convinced those bills were inside the vehicle and we were going to find them. Out came the back seat. Next the door panels. First the front, then the left rear. "Whadaya know," I bellowed. "Look here."

There they were. My flashlight probing into the dark space behind the door panel revealed six $20.00 bills. Three hours of searching and we had confirmed our suspicions. I must admit that my confidence we would find the money had started to wane a teensy bit toward the end, but my faith in the ingenuity of most poachers kept me going.

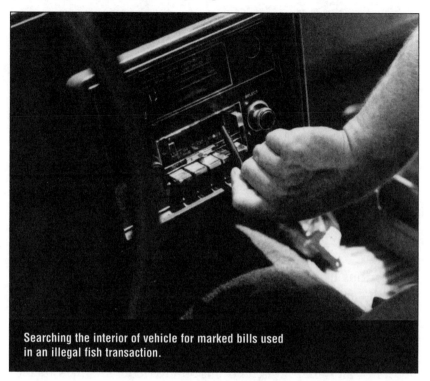

Searching the interior of vehicle for marked bills used in an illegal fish transaction.

We had half; where was the other half? Our attitudes were now more positive. It was just a matter of time. Finally, my partner, with screwdriver in hand, exclaimed, "Here's the rest of it." Between the cassette player and the dash frame was a small space. Each of the other six bills had been individually pushed into this narrow gap, totally invisible unless the whole unit was removed. This most likely explained the movement we had observed inside the car during the chase. They had shoved the bills into the door through a small slit in the vinyl next to the ashtray, again completely undetectable to the eye.

The outcome of the case? All four suspects were sentenced to a month of education at the local community college with evenings spent at the jail. No fines! A great application of alternative sentencing.

TWELVE

The Creepy Ambush

S erious fish poachers have always applied their cunning to the fabrication of illegal contraptions designed to effectively take fish. Most of these homemade devices have two things in common: they are easily disguised and they're cheap. Meticulously constructed steel mesh traps, five-to-eight tined spears of all dimensions, and false-bottomed containers including modified gas tanks for hiding illegal catches are examples of devices constructed by fish poachers. Some appliances are even made at shops and places of employment during working hours. In some communities there appears to be no shame in this brand of behavior which is occasionally even encouraged by fellow employees. The reluctance to inform on these people has much to do with being branded a stoolie in one's own workplace. Even folks that are otherwise good resource stewards make a decision to close their eyes to the goings-on. This is one reason it's so difficult for an officer to generate significant documentation of violations, especially when the activities are done on or near private lands.

Spawning game fish that congregate near the shores and shallows of our lakes and creeks during the spring run are the normal targets of these delinquents armed with their crude gadgets. With little information, the only tools an officer can employ in combating this form of treachery are constant patrolling and surveillance of known violation areas and applying years of experience to identify the most probable locations of potential violations.

I knew that trapping spawning game fish in many of the county's numerous rivers and creeks was a spring ritual for various rural residents. This is another example of a hand-me-down pastime that is a function of location and family customs. Most likely more than one generation has used these same sites to acquire out-of-season fillets. Smaller rivers that form tributaries to larger waterways are the most likely places for a fish trap. On a normal year when the water levels begin to recede from the spring runoff, the spawning fish will swim upstream along the banks of these slower moving waters, deposit their eggs, and return to the larger and deeper waters of the river system.

The Swan River south of Grand Rapids was such a place and became the focus of my attention for this particular spring's work. A warm Friday afternoon in late April drew me to a spot that I had worked for six years without success. The final 10 miles of the snaking river before it emptied into the Mississippi consisted of hard-to-access banks that were either bordering private land or required a long trek through forested lowlands and swamps. The only method to survey the remote shorelines was to paddle quietly by canoe, inspecting the muddy edges for wires or fresh human disruptions of dead vegetation.

As a fellow officer and I studied the first five miles, my partner spotted a small wire emerging from the water. As I grasped the wire from the stern, I could feel pressure pulling from the deeper water behind the canoe. Unable to move the weight to which the wire was connected, we both climbed ashore and pulled. Slowly, a rusty, weed-covered object that resembled a mesh-like barrel appeared out of the dark water. It was exactly what we were looking for, a large homemade fish trap. I immediately looked around to confirm we hadn't been detected and then calculated our location. There were no fish in the trap at this time, so we submerged it again and checked the area above the 6-foot bank. A narrow hay field bordered the river and led directly to a county road about a quarter mile to the east. I was familiar with the setting and had long suspected the party living in the residence adjacent to the field. "Let's get out of here," I whispered. "We'll set up for tomorrow. Looks like they already checked the trap today. This is a good one!" We continued our patrol the next five miles to our waiting vehicle, loaded up and drove back to town for a long-awaited meal and discussion of future strategy.

Scanty third-party information at best had brought me to this location six years before. This small farm was situated at the end of a two-mile dead-end road. It was impossible to get anywhere near the residence or adjoining river by any type of vehicle without being seen. Any "stranger" would surely be identified, thus negating any enforcement effort. It was a perfect place for violating the game and fish laws. One mile to the east was the closest "friendly" residence that I could count on for an entry site. Over the last six years, I had made five visits to the suspect location using this place as my starting point. The hike involved a quarter-mile slog through a dense cedar swamp. Sloshing and dragging my soaked feet through this nasty quagmire only reminded me that I also had to face a return trip. My former excursions had led me to an old rusty fish trap on this particular "forty" about 300 yards from a residence and hidden in the brush just above the stream bank. This kept my interest alive and explains why I continued to monitor the area. I thought one of these times I'd get lucky. Hopefully, this was the year.

I shifted into gear and planned my next morning. My usual partner couldn't help me, but a fellow officer friend from southern Minnesota had called the week before and offered his assistance on the coming weekend. This was perfect. We had something to target while he was here.

When Gary arrived, I told him of my plan of attack. He was a terrific guy open to any challenge and was not averse to our swamp march the next morning.

After our tramp through no-man's land, we slumped down in the brush at the edge of the road and took a breather. It was a beautiful morning with the sun just beginning to warm the chilled air as it rose above the pine and birch horizon. I explained to Gary how the narrow field across the road led directly to the trapping site.

We both agreed that getting there unobserved was going to be a real test of our stealth capability. The house windows faced the field, and anyone near the trap would likely spot us during our trip through the alfalfa. The only thing in our favor was the contour of the field itself. It had a wide hump near the river that would hide our approach as long as we were on our bellies. We would also be obscured from the house due to a small hedge lining the driveway.

"Let's go for it," I proposed to Gary. "If no one is there, at least we'll have a good surveillance position for the rest of the day."

Off we crept with binoculars dragging. Four hundred yards to go. Two hundred yards, one hundred. "Let's rest a minute and take a look." I raised myself up on my elbows and peered through the glasses. Instantly I dropped flat.

"Somebody's there, just over the hill," I muttered. "Let's crawl a little closer just to the bottom of the rise."

Gary was no less keyed up than I was. After all these years there was finally a chance to apply some strong enforcement, I thought, as we inched closer and closer. Only 50 feet from the bank, we could hear voices just beyond the peak.

"There's two of them, Gary. I think we should crawl a little farther and just stand up and approach them. Whatdaya think?"

"Sounds like a plan," Gary panted in anticipation. "Let's go."

It's always a rush to walk up undetected on folks who may be violating. The most important thing is to take control and observe as much as possible during those first few seconds of contact.

As we stood up, we immediately encountered a scene that confirmed our suspicions and was about to close a chapter on fish poaching in this area—they were filleting northern pike on a cleaning table next to a freshly pulled fish trap. I thought, as we tiptoed up behind them, "All the effort and hours over all those years . . . finally." Now within three feet, we were both amazed how intent they were at stripping the meat from the skin that they didn't detect our presence.

"Good morning, fellas. How's fishing?"

Both of the middle-aged men turned in unison with fillet knives in hand and mouths open, staring at our uniforms.

"Why don't you just put the knives down and stand where you are," I instructed.

"Looks like we may have a situation here. How about producing some identification?"

Neither of them said anything as they nervously reached for their wallets. I doubt if they were yet capable of communicating due to the shock of the moment. After retrieving the fillet knives and creating a safe situation, we inspected the evidence: a large homemade 5-foot-long, 3-foot-diameter fish trap that we had discovered the afternoon before, knives, fillet boards, bags and fish—all northern pike. About six fish out of a dozen were lying on the ground yet to be cleaned. I realized we had just made it. Another half hour and they would have been gone. Good timing and good luck on our part.

Both of the gentlemen were courteous. Of course, there's something to be said about scaring the bejesus out of the violator to guarantee cooperation. I immediately recognized one of the poachers. He was the person who lived in the nearby dwelling and to whom I had devoted much of my time (and swamp walks) pursuing. Definitely there was some satisfaction here considering that trapping or netting fish is a gross misdemeanor and that he would have to go before "The Hanging Judge," a label that was tagged on a local district judge who was less than sympathetic when it came to administering justice to game and fish violators. The second perpetrator was a person I didn't know but who turned out to be a local educator. This was a sad state of affairs when you assume that all of your kids' teachers have at least a minimum of ethical and moral values. Further searching on the property revealed no less than four more elaborate traps hidden in various bushes along the bank and well out of sight from recreational users on the river.

A sad note: Less than six years later, Conservation Officer Gary Wesby was tragically killed in a car accident in his home town. He is missed.

Officer Gary Wesby with homemade fish traps pulled from a local river during the spring fish run.

THIRTEEN
The Chevy Chase

A game warden's involvement in cases unrelated to game and fish is small even though, as peace officers, they are authorized to make arrests on all statute violations. Many of the non-resource incidents that are encountered by game wardens stem from investigations and apprehensions of game and fish or recreational violators.

Much duck and goose hunting enforcement during the first few weeks of the season involves combating after-hours shooting. For decades, the migratory waterfowl hunting regulations have restricted hunters from taking ducks and geese after 4:00 p.m. the first three weeks of the season. This rule and most of the other laws controlling the taking of migratory waterfowl are set in conjunction with the U.S. Fish and Wildlife Department options that are implemented by each state. The 4:00 p.m. closing has always had its critics, but by and large most hunters accept the rule and view it as a way of providing the local ducks a time of rest during the early migration.

On a calm overcast afternoon in October, I took up a position at a public boat access in a well-known duck area near a power plant that towers above a 4-square-mile expanse of water. This setting is inundated with bulrushes and wild rice that form a myriad of pathways for hunters to gain entry and build blinds and set decoys to attract ducks. This expanse of the Mississippi River is a perfect environment for attracting waterfowl and for providing the local hunters an opportunity to pursue local and early migrant ducks before freeze-up. My purpose was to monitor any "late shooting" after closed hours and try to pinpoint the location of the muffled shots. This would give me an idea of the extent of the illegal activity and provide me with an agenda for the next afternoon's work on the water.

About 4:30 I heard an approaching engine noise coming from a nearby clearing that surrounded the town's water tower. The sound increased until I finally spotted a small passenger car slowly emerging from the gated area. For a moment I thought it a bit strange for anyone to be back there but didn't give it a great deal of thought since my attention was directed at the river and I was listening intently for shots. As I glanced again toward the little sedan advancing 50 feet away, the driver's eyes locked on my uniform—instantly the car hit full acceleration as its wheels spun in the gravel and the high-pitched whine of the tiny engine propelled it due west down an asphalt straightaway. No doubt this guy was not in the mood to chat, and his intentions were clear . . . leave the scene and put distance between us.

Instinctively, I jumped into my patrol truck and headed out after him. So far no violation had been witnessed, but the driver's conduct certainly necessitated my further scrutiny.

"I'll just get up behind him and follow," I thought. "Maybe he'll blow a stop sign or commit a moving violation of some sort and give me cause to at least stop him and check him out." I noted our speed increasing to 75 miles per hour.

"This guy's accelerating. This isn't going to be a typical stop. I believe I'm in a chase with a compact rust-bucket. With the looming highway and the high speed, I think I'm going to need some help here," I mumbled to myself as we approached a "T" intersection. Whoosh! Running that stop sign justified my further pursuit as my "pursuee" began disregarding most of the traffic codes and headed into the town of Cohasset.

At this speed, steering with one hand and clutching the mike in the other to call dispatch while flying across a set of railroad tracks and squealing through the parking lots of a bar and post office were creating a real challenge. Always on my mind was the safety of the public so I tried to be visually aware of everything around me.

"Dispatch, I'm in pursuit of a small yellow sedan now southbound across the Mississippi River in Cohasset. Do you have anybody near?" I yelled into the radio as I kicked the throttle down.

"Whatcha got, Tom?" came a familiar voice. It was another Tom, the highway patrolman.

"I've got one running. Don't know why. I'm southbound about halfway to the cemetery."

"I'm about three miles away. I'll head over there. Keep me informed on your location."

I was now about 300 yards behind the car as it approached another "T" intersection. The roads ahead were very narrow and winding, and I was worried more about safety than anything. At this speed, red lights and sirens aren't a sufficient warning system for others unaware of what's happening. Just as I was letting up, the car made a complete u-turn and was now headed straight back in my direction. I had to make an instant decision: let him go by and start the pursuit all over again or just not give him room to get around me. It wouldn't be the first time I took a vehicle head-on, but those occasions were at night and all of them had stopped. I decided to block the entire road. Just as I pulled in his lane and slowed, the little menace took a sharp right, bounced through the ditch taking out two mailboxes, and ground his way across the front lawn of a residence to jump back on the road behind me.

Now I was really energized. The adrenalin was surging and I knew it, but I just had to stay calm and rely on help.

"Tom, if you're out there, he's coming your way. Should be on Highway 2 in about one minute."

From the time it took me to turn around, my suspect was almost out of sight, turning right toward Highway 2.

"I'm just about there," Tom replied, as I punched the accelerator to the floor again.

I caught up enough to see the vehicle speed across all four lanes of Highway 2 without slowing or looking. "Now we have a public safety issue," I said to myself. "This guy's gotta be stopped."

As I eased across the same highway, I could see State Patrolman Tom approaching from the east.

"Keep on him. I'll get behind you," he hollered.

Now the three of us were northbound on County Road 62. I, 100 feet behind the violator and Tom, 100 feet behind me. This appeared to be getting out of control—as if I was ever in control since the whole thing started. This road would wind for another 12 miles before the next intersection. We both knew that this could go on for a long time, that it could put others in jeopardy and, the worst scenario, that somebody could get hurt. Now at top speeds of 70 to 75 miles per hour, our culprit was negotiating curves on the wrong side and showed no signs of giving up.

"This is ridiculous," said Tom. "I'll call the Captain and get permission to take him out."

"I'll just stay with him then until we hear," I sounded back.

After describing the situation to the patrol captain, we both heard, "Don't let him go any farther. He's going to hurt somebody. Run him off."

About a mile from the intersection and 12 miles into the chase, Tom directed me to tap the left rear bumper. This should be enough on the dusty gravel road to spin the car around, forcing it to lose control and hopefully coming to rest against the outside ditch bank.

As I gently touched my right front bumper to the speeder's left rear bumper, I accelerated and then let up on the gas. I watched in anticipation as the sedan did a complete 360 spin-out, skidding sideways toward the shallow ditch, ricocheting off some small saplings and finally sliding to a standstill on the outside bank of the depression.

"Whew," I thought. "Nobody hurt and we got the son-of-a-gun stopped."

At that point, a deputy sheriff appeared from the north as Tom and I approached the driver. The offender was out of his vehicle with an ugly, "Want to fight?" attitude. I'm really glad there were three of us at the scene because this boy didn't want to submit easily. He was pumped and had no intentions of going to jail without some strong motivation—force and handcuffs.

The other officers and I immediately recognized with whom we were dealing. Hand restraints were no stranger to this individual. Although I knew him as a career poacher, the other officers were also well aware of his past nongame felonies and driving transgressions.

Now some of my questions could be answered. Just exactly why was he running? What was in the vehicle? Did it have to do with poaching? With a lack of cooperation on the defendant's part, I could only guess what his intentions might have been. In the vehicle was a custom-made 30.06 scoped rifle with a thick diameter bull barrel. This person had been arrested eight years earlier by my neighboring officer with more than a dozen deer in possession out of season. I can only assume he was hunting before season when I first spotted his vehicle exiting an area that is known to contain large numbers of deer. Further investigation of that spot revealed nothing related to a shot deer, however. I assume he failed to spot a deer to shoot on this particular trip. His reason for evasion most likely had to do with a revoked driver's license, expired plates and felony probation.

Even though there were strong clues that illegal hunting was most likely taking place that day, the gentleman was never charged with a game violation. There simply wasn't the circumstantial evidence necessary for a charge. I regretted that the gun, which I suspected had taken and would probably continue to take numerous illegal animals, had to be returned. But as one of the deputies in charge confided to me later, "Tom, I don't think you have to worry about that rifle ever shooting straight again."

FOURTEEN
The Faulty Success

The type of relationship a conservation officer shares with the resort community in his area is all-important when it comes to ensuring an adequate level of fishing enforcement, which in turn provides an equal playing field for legal sportsmen. The owners and operators of private resorts are the frontline observers capable of providing a range of facts and information so very valuable for protecting the resource on their individual lakes. However, the resorter is walking a financial and business tightrope when a choice has to be made between exposing an in-house violation or looking the other way. Economically, a minimal, short-term loss is possible if the particular guest involved is the type that would be resentful and fail to rebook. However, it wouldn't take long for the word to circulate that illegal behavior involving fish violations is something that is not tolerated or condoned by management. If this simple premise would be championed by the entire resort community, it can be almost guaranteed that the violation rate would decline and fair-play concerns would decrease. Added bonuses would include a better quality of client in the future, more than making up for the small initial loss and creating a feeling of trust that would eventually permeate the clientele. This philosophy seems to be more of a pipe dream than reality, but it does express a standard for the long-term protection of our resource.

I must say that the resort owners in the areas I was assigned were on the whole, good, hardworking folks who knew the importance of promoting respect for the game and the laws that in turn protected the very resource upon which their businesses depended. A few had to be enlightened occasionally by an enforcement action, but this also provided another chance to educate.

On Lake Winnibigoshish, 12 resorts dot the shoreline of this 58,000 acre impoundment. Another six sit along the shores of Bowstring Lake to the east, both lakes being prime walleye habitat. I kept a personal mental rating of all my resorts—a one on the scale signifying the worst of attitudes and a ten suggesting a premium mindset and approach dealing with resource violations. A few personal contacts with the owners would inform me precisely where they stood on enforcement issues. Of course, the lower the rating, the more effort I would put into those locations. The following account is one of many cases that supported this theory.

The initial call came in about 6:00 p.m. in the middle of the week. The informant's voice was immediately familiar and one with whom I'd had much contact during our 25-five year association. "Tom, think I have a good one for you here. A couple of personal 16-footers are filling up out here, and they need to be checked. Are you available?" he inquired in anticipation.

"You bet! What's the story?"

"Should be four guys in two Lund boats, both with Iowa stickers. Already watched them take a limit and they're back out again. I would guess they'll be returning at dark or just after. Pretty sure they're renting cabin 10."

"OK I'll head up and take it from here. Thanks!" These types of calls weren't that unusual, and more often than I want to admit, resulted in a failed attempt to locate or confront the would-be perpetrators. However, I had much more faith in this call due to the status of the informant. He was a trained observer and an enthusiastic supporter of conservation officers' enforcement efforts. Besides, he was calling on clients of a resort that I rated about a "two" on my resort-attitude scale. The resort owner just had no interest in his patrons' actions and felt little responsibility for promoting honesty or compliance with the fishing laws.

I arrived just as the sun was setting. Hopefully, I wasn't late and the folks in question were still out fishing. I would need permission to enter their living quarters, so it was important for me to see them arrive at the docks and watch them proceed to their cabin. The place was very busy, boats and fishermen arriving every minute, parking their crafts, and strolling in all directions among the cabins, the fish cleaning house and the lodge. I strained to see the boat stickers from a perch on a hill overlooking much of the facility. My binoculars only had another 15 minutes of light-gathering capabilities before they would become useless for any further identification.

Just at dark, I recognized a boat with an Iowa license attaching to my side of a dock. The two occupants eventually unloaded some gear, secured the ropes and headed for the row of cabins. I struggled to follow their course, moving out of sight and parallel to the path until I could see which cabin they were about to enter. Cabin 10! I knew I would have to get permission to go in, so I really had no choice but to question the last person through the door.

"Excuse me, sir. Game warden. Just checking fish success tonight. Kind of a hurry. Mind if I have a look in your freezer there? Got a lot of other cabins to check so I'd appreciate your permission to make sure everything's legal here."

"Yeah, I guess so. Hey, guys, warden wants to check our fish," he anxiously called to his two buddies.

"Go ahead. Fish are in there," as he pointed at the refrigerator in the corner. I quickly inspected the freezer and the refrigerator compartments. Both contained frozen and semi-frozen fillets of walleyes far over the possession limit for four people. "How many are staying here? How many in your party?" I inquired.

"There's four of us. The other two are still out fishing."

That certainly confirmed my information so I continued my strategy. "Looks like you have a few too many fish here. Let's all walk down together to your boat and check the live well. C'mon, let's go!"

Reluctantly, all three followed my instructions and marched awkwardly down the path to the moored boat. As I suspected, there were more fish floating in the box ready to be cleaned. My next tactic was to get us all back to the cabin so as not to alert the other two in the group of my presence. I cautioned both to refrain from using their cell phones until I could talk to their two friends. They complied but were getting more and more nervous as the minutes ticked by. About ten minutes later, footsteps were heard approaching and in walked two men who quickly recognized the situation.

"Game warden. Just checking fish tonight. Let's all go down to your boat and check your live-well, please." I ordered.

Little was said among the four on our second trip to the dock. Inside the boat's fish tank were yet more swimming walleyes destined for the fillet board. These increased the total to more than 45 fish, well over the 24 fish possession limit for four people. And this was only the middle of the week.

Even though summonses were written and their fish seized, what is most noteworthy is that the four people were complete gentlemen and cooperated with every part of the process.

My phone rang about noon the next day. It was my informant. I was sure he was about to congratulate my successful effort spawned by his accurate facts that helped bring a good over-limit fish case to conclusion. In fact, that was the case. "Good job, Tom. Heard all about it early this morning. The place was buzzing last night. I was up there early this morning, and I think you made quite an impact. Hopefully a deterrent for the others."

"Thanks, buddy. Couldn't have done it without you," I affirmed.

"There's one more thing I think you should know, however."

"What's that?"

"You got the wrong guys!!"

"What! You want to repeat that?" I said, thinking this was poor timing for a joke.

"Really. I gave you the wrong cabin number. The boys I suspected came in well after dark, a long time after your contacts with those guys. You got the wrong group."

"You mean there was another group of four from Iowa that were the actual suspects? What are the chances!"

"That's what I'm saying, Tom. Good job, but four more got away. They left this morning. Kinda tells ya how much is going on around here, doesn't it."

After I was satisfied this actually happened, I dutifully thanked him again and sat back to ponder the whole state of affairs. The likelihood of this phenomenon is higher than most people might think in the business of game and fish enforcement. That's the scary part. The random discoveries of illegal game and fish has happened too many times for them not to be taken seriously. I've come across these random conditions during investigations no less than half-a-dozen times and always marvel at the potential for major poaching that could possibly be taking place right under our noses. It certainly confirms the need for folks to be vigilant concerning this type of behavior and for resort owners to uphold standards on their properties.

FIFTEEN
The Lesson Not Learned

Developing a strategy on where and when to work during the busiest times of the year relies as much on help from the public as it does on an officer's own intuition. Both are really intertwined since a game warden's instinctive path is many times dictated by the information supplied by the sportsmen for whom they work. That's why TIP or Turn In Poachers, a nonprofit private organization that helps channel information on wildlife violation to the proper field agent, is so very necessary in the functioning of any enforcement organization. TIP provides a conduit for concerned citizens to supply information on any resource abuse and at the same time remain anonymous. Hopefully, most citizens feel comfortable with this arrangement and are willing to furnish hints on poaching activity that wardens so desperately need to do their job more efficiently.

One of my neighboring officers received an anonymous call one year on the second day of deer season that a possible overlimit of mallard ducks had been shot the day before on a small, remote lake. His investigation led him to a camp about a half mile off a county road where he discovered some evidence that supported the TIP call. The hunters appeared to have closed up the small trailer and left for the season.

Putting this info on the back burner, Denny called the next fall and asked me for help in following up on the case. It was somewhat out of the ordinary to focus on duck hunters on the opening day of deer season; however, poachers are also aware of this and don't hesitate to adjust their operations.

The narrow rutty trail through the woods emptied into a 2-acre clearing with a stark, weather-beaten 30-foot trailer house parked at one end. Immediately in our view from the forest edge we saw what appeared to be a row of severed mallard heads strung out evenly along a clothesline that ended at a white cleaning table. A 5-minute surveillance revealed no signs of life in or around the trailer. As we approached, the sight of fresh feathers and duck parts supported our belief that the hunters had most likely hunted the day before deer season, not the opening day as was assumed from the information the year before.

Finding no one at the trailer, we felt certain that they were out hunting deer or ducks. After searching the wooded area surrounding the camp, Denny found a man in his 20s on a deer stand not far into the woods. After explaining our mission, we walked with the cooperative gentleman back to the clearing and into the trailer house. Amazingly, the first words from his mouth struck us as being a bit out of context: "I know what you guys want. You're probably looking for our ducks, As you're going to see, we shot too many! I just graduated from conservation officer school in Ely. Is this going to affect my chances for a job?"

Incredulous, we both stared at each other and marveled at this guy's direct admissions and then almost in unison replied, "Yes, sir, this will definitely have a negative effect on your employment chances with our department. We'd also suggest not wasting your time applying for a natural resource enforcement job. In other words, you will definitely have to modify your career goals!" It was a bit comical, but we put the little inquiry to rest.

Next came the inspection of the game on the premises and interrogation of the young man as to licensing and other hunters in camp.

"My hunting partner is still out deer hunting but should be back anytime," he said.

Denny remained inside as he questioned the young man further about the previous year and other possible illegal game and fish involvements. I went outside and started to identify and count the dressed ducks that were contained in two coolers and to inspect the undressed ducks, some of which were still on the cleaning table. Suddenly, the faint noise of an engine could be heard approaching from the right side of the trailer. As the engine whine increased, I crept over to the corner and waited. The slowly creeping three-wheel ATV was within 5 feet of the trailer's edge when I stepped out directly in its path. Now, this was a scene neither of us ever anticipated. The first thing I saw was the hunter's face. His eyes as big as saucers revealed an expression of instant dread. I most likely looked much the same to him. When a person is shocked that intensely, the shocker also becomes a bit shaken. There I stood in full uniform two feet from an individual who was flaunting at least two observable violations. Over his shoulder was strapped an uncased, loaded rifle, and flopped over the back of the ATV was an untagged small buck deer.

"Just here to check your licenses," I said in a controlled voice. "Whatcha got here?"

Little emotion emanated from this young man other than a stare of nervous resignation. After inspecting the gun and deer, I directed him back to the trailer where we started the appropriate paperwork.

You would think that the enforcement action taken that day would be ample to provide a deterrent to future illegal behavior. The summonses issued included two over-limits of migratory waterfowl. They had eighteen ducks and only two per hunter was the limit that year; an unplugged shotgun (it's a federal offense to take migratory waterfowl with a firearm capable of holding more than three shells); no small game license; transporting an untagged deer; loss of hunting privileges for one of them; and a number of warning tickets on other violations. Most folks who are caught violating the game and fish laws submit to the fines and other penalties imposed and often engage in future positive behavior. A few, however, resist these deterrent measures and need to have a higher level of penalty imposed in

Illegal duck camp discovered in remote woods.

order to change their outdoor conduct. This type of hunter is still in what is called the "shooting stage" of hunter maturity. No matter what their age, they just haven't progressed to a more idealistic sporting attitude and are still stuck in the phase where killing and getting the limit—or more—is the driving force in their hunting careers. Thankfully, most hunters do mature to the "method" and "trophy" stages, eventually winding up in the "sportsman" stage, which is the ultimate point where nature, friends and exercise are the fundamental reasons for hunting.

Sadly, that was not the situation in this case. The following year, one of the individuals was caught poaching ducks on the same lake and using an unplugged shotgun. Within a few years he was again caught with an over-limit of northern pike. Finally, his partner was caught seven years later shining deer in no less auspicious a location than Fort Snelling National Cemetery in the Twin Cities. This constituted a gross misdemeanor with loss of hunting privileges for three years. Loss of privileges has proven to be the most effective deterrent on people that are habitual violators. As some of these people get older, there is always the hope that a few will look back and possibly see the light. For the benefit of all the legal sportsmen, one can only hope!

SIXTEEN
The Bear Facts

A game warden can pretty much be assured that any nuisance animal complaint holds a high degree of likelihood that a major malfunction will happen, particularly if the beast in question has to be dealt with directly. Wild animals, being high strung by nature, tend to behave in a manner not consistent with the plans to save or contain the creature for its own good. Each creature has its own unique threshold of anxiety and will behave accordingly. I doubt if a game warden exists who hasn't experienced a situation where one or more of these animals has created an embarrassing and awkward moment. Any animal control officer in the country could grip a crowd with stories of insignificant little creatures holding groups of grown men at bay for hours.

Although I've dealt with many of these critters over time, by far the most captivating and unpredictable was the black bear. Thanks to a change in policy in the 1990s, officers are no longer required to deal with bear complaints. But prior to the '90s there were summers when the bear intrusions into populated areas would stifle an officer's normal game and fish enforcement work by 50 percent. Most of the grumbling was from people who didn't know that their bird feeders could attract a bear from a mile away. Education seemed to help, but we still had to deal with "There's a bear in my yard" calls repeatedly.

One incident involved a hasty decision on my part. I was transporting a tranquilized bear through town and decided to get a quick bite at my residence. (Game wardens occasionally drugged bears as a last resort in those years.) Parking in the alley, I slid the snoring bulk of muscle from the bed of the pickup to the front seat of my personal truck so it would be out of sight. I didn't want unsuspecting kids walking by to discover a sleepy bruin and create a scene. I rolled the window down a couple inches and went to make myself a sandwich. I figured I had a half hour to eat since the dosage guaranteed a sleep cycle of at least another hour and a half.

It turned out to be one of the dumbest moves I've ever made (other than maybe taking a pitiful shot at a treed bear's hind end followed by the thud of a tranquilizer dart impacting the roof of the complainant's house, or blowing a beaver dam under a very obvious powerline, causing a three-hour electrical failure for a 40-mile stretch from Nashwauk to Togo). Anyway, as I approached my pickup, something seemed amiss. The windows were totally steamed up and the truck cab was shaking. As I ran up to the driver's window and looked through the blurred slobber, I was met with a massive pink tongue parked between a set of brown-stained chattering teeth. So much for the drug estimate. Besides the strings of drool being tossed from side-to-side, the pungent odor radiating from the 2-inch gap was stomach-churning. Glancing at my former front seat, it became obvious that bears don't necessarily just do it in the woods!

My presence didn't exactly calm the now fully enraged black hair ball. He started attacking the window with his 2-inch clawed paws while spitting and hissing with each irritated strike. "Gentle Ben" was upset. He wanted out, and I had no doubt he would eventually accomplish that goal with or without me opening a door. The more he came unglued, the larger the chunks of seat padding were seen free floating inside the trashed cab. Whoa . . . there goes a hunk of my dashboard. "No way am I turning this in to my insurance agent," I thought as two younger guys walked by.

"How's it goin', Tom?"

"OK! Just headin' back to work. Take care," I said as I feigned a walk toward my patrol truck. Good. Got rid of those would-be witnesses. I've got to think of something here! There really weren't lots of options. I could dart him again but that would most likely prove fatal. Or I could let him out right here and hope for the best. After all, he was in town when I captured him, so we'd just be back to square one. I grabbed the handle and gently pulled on the door. He immediately saw the daylight, and before I could step back, his entire hulk exploded out of the side of the truck, ramming the door against my face. He was heading for the middle school. Little concern since there was no school in session, but I was sure it would only be minutes before the first call: "Just saw a bear running north along First Avenue." Incredibly, no call came that day. My next day off, however, was dedicated to restoring, refurbishing, reconditioning or otherwise rebuilding the interior of my truck. I started with a hose.

While heading north of Grand Rapids at about 10:00 a.m. on a sunny Saturday morning, local dispatch informed me of yet another bear heading south from the fairgrounds and asked if I would be interested in monitoring its route.

"Yeah, I'll take a look," I replied indifferently. After all, bears were all over town that year and little could be done to steer it in a precise direction. But, being the one who was expected to be in charge of things like this, I turned in that direction. There it was. A fairly good-size bear jogging south—right toward my residence.

"That's odd," I thought as I slowly idled along behind the lumbering critter and watched it run straight into my yard. My unsuspecting 6-year-old daughter was sitting on the edge of the sandbox when I witnessed her bewilderment as the big black bear leaped over her sand pile and dashed southwest out of the yard.

"What are the chances?" I pondered. "A bear flat-out through the warden's backyard and my daughter as a witness." I'm sure the thing was gone before it registered with her as to what sort of companion she had momentarily shared her play area with. I was relieved that a collision was averted, but mixed emotions of anxiety and relief hung with me the rest of the day. Now that I had him in my sights, I would just continue the little pursuit and try to escort him out of town before the next call came in. "Now it's southbound on Highway 38," I shouted into the mike. "Oops. Now he's up on the first floor roof of a house peering in the upstairs window."

I met with the local PD (police department) car, and we both watched as the bear pawed the window. Failing in that attempt, it finally climbed down the rain gutter, jumped on the hood of a car in its rapid descent to the ground, leaving scratches in the paint, and ultimately scampered into the path of U.S. Highway 2 traffic. The approaching cars and trucks slammed on their brakes as our bear, oblivious to its own danger, marched across the busy intersection, over the railroad tracks and toward a block of businesses. It paused in front of a department store, then raised up on its hind feet and scratched at the glass, appearing to study the window display. A moment later it sprinted down the sidewalk, and I watched in alarm as the keyed-up beast headed directly for a daydreaming young boy riding a bicycle.

"This isn't going to be good," I thought. Just as the bear was 20 feet away, the youngster looked up in a panic and instantly threw his bike to the ground as the brute burst past him on its way to the gates of the local paper mill. A penny for the boy's thoughts!

As I proceeded to the gate, out of nowhere, an individual on crutches in a full leg cast appeared in front of my car. I came to a stop as he hobbled up along side and jumped on my hood. "Let's go," he shouted. "Let's follow the bear."

Not knowing who he was but not wanting to lose sight of the bear, I continued my expedition with this broken-legged stranger as my hood ornament, cast protruding straight out the front of the grill. As we entered the gate and worked our way through the maze of buildings, some of the employees glanced in amazement as this bizarre parade of critter, cast and car rumbled by and into the wood yard. One of the workers finally noticed the approaching bear as he was maneuvering a pike pole to adjust the stacks of logs. He instinctively held the long pole straight out as a defense weapon while the animal leaped over a pile of logs only feet away. Stunned, the man took off around the large mountain of pulp and watched as the bear jumped into the adjacent Mississippi River and swam to the opposite shore. As it crawled up the bank and ran across a lawn, it was the end of the line for our bear quest. "Best to you, bear," I reflected. "You deserve a rest and please don't stop for lunch on your way out of town."

To this day I have no idea why there was any need to trail this particular bear in the manner described. I suppose it has a little to do with the chase instinct imprinted in our genes long ago. A wild animal call to a warden generally reflects civilization's fear of the natural world. Just think how much fear the citizens of the natural world feel when invaded by civilization.

SEVENTEEN
The Shady Deal

The clear deep waters of Pokegama Lake, a few miles south of Grand Rapids, stretch for 12 miles passing through Little and Big Jay Gould Lakes, eventually pouring into the Mississippi River in the town of Cohasset. This rich basin of backwater lying upstream from the Pokegama Dam is home to many species of fish including walleyes, bass, lake trout and a supply of large northern pike that have been well fed over the last 25 years due to the illegal introduction of smelt, a highly nutritious forage fish.

Most of the shoreland owners who fish and recreate on these lakes realize the uniqueness and value of the area. That's why it was hard for me to understand the extent to which some of the residents would go to abuse the very resource that was so near and dear to them.

I had long suspected a Pokegama landowner who lived in a plush home on the south end of the lake of illegally gill-netting game fish such as northern pike in the fall. A gill net can be used legally at this time but only to catch nongame species such as whitefish, tullibees and suckers. From the information I had gathered over five years, this person would intentionally set for the game fish by placing his nets in water over the 6-foot maximum depth allowed by the rules, thereby increasing the chances of snaring the more sought-after northern pike.

I always felt it worth my time to try to catch these types of folks who so deliberately exploited the resource.

Finally, the opportunity came for me to set my own nets to put an end to his poaching. On an early spring afternoon at the local Department of Natural Resources (DNR) regional service center, I was approaching my patrol truck in the parking lot and noticed a man reaching in through my driver's window and then walking away. Immediately I saw that my sunglasses were missing from the front seat and decided to follow the guy around and into the back of the main building. Squaring off with him just inside the door, I could see my glasses sticking out of his shirt pocket. "You seem to have acquired some pretty cool Bausch and Lombs," I said casually. I knew him as a regular employee, and we always had gotten along well over the years. Plucking the glasses from his shirt, I uttered a few words of disappointment that he would violate our friendship and ended with a few remarks on how this little theft infraction could certainly jeopardize his work status and even his job. He was sweating and he was scared!

Then the bells went off; I remembered that my friend was a neighbor to my favorite Pokegama Lake illegal gill-netter. I thought, "No better chance than now. Let's tighten the screws just a little further for the State of Minnesota." I told him that there might be a way to lessen his anxiety and make amends on his thieving. "You're a neighbor to a fish violator on Pokegama, aren't you?" I queried. He immediately named the individual to whom I was referring, giving me even a greater sense that the poacher was worth pursuing.

My light-fingered buddy said, "I suppose you're talkin' about all those illegal fish he takes."

"Yup," I said. "That's the guy. How about you help me catch him. I've been trying for years, but I never know when he goes out. It's all in the timing, you know. Let's put it this way;

I'll make you a deal. You supply me with something that will help me catch the guy in the next year, and this little sunglass infraction will be put away for good. Whatdaya think?"

It didn't take long for my little buddy to strike a deal. He was hurtin' and he knew it.

"Yeah, I'll do what I can. I know what he's been up to."

"All right," I said. "I'll be waiting. Remember now, you owe me!"

His demeanor improved as he walked away, most likely due to the fact he would be going home with his job intact. My gut feelings were that there was a likely chance this little bargain had some potential.

The following November, an evening phone call revealed a familiar, somewhat quaky voice; "Tom, I think I got what you need. They're going out tomorrow morning."

I quickly realized it was my sunglasses buddy and that he was making good on our little contract. "Great," I said. "What time and exactly where?"

"There'll be two, just out in front of their place right after sunrise."

"Thanks. I'll see what I can do. Talk to you later."

I immediately got into gear and called my neighboring officer to the west. Willy was always willing to help on a moment's notice, and we planned to arrive at the scene around 5:30 a.m.

We parked our vehicle a quarter mile from the residence in question and walked to a brushy site on a 30-foot hill overlooking the beach where the suspects would most likely take to the water. As it started to get light, an eerie, fog-laden scene emerged, pierced only by the plaintive cry of a distant loon. The only boat visible was an overturned 14-footer lying below us at the bottom of the hill about 10 feet from the water's edge. Not knowing if the suspects had yet gone out, were already on the water, or had decided not to net this particular morning, we sat silently and waited and watched. Even with the coming of full light, the fog was so impenetrable that we could barely see 30 feet off shore.

After 15 minutes, when we were about as comfortable as we could get in the 30-degree chill, a sound of an oar slightly tapping the gunwales of a boat broke the silence. Moments later we could also hear the slurping of water dipped by the oars of the approaching boat. Cautiously we both moved into position, peering in the direction of the noise and eagerly awaited any trace of movement from the ghostly waters just offshore. "There they are, Willy! They're about 40 feet out." The bow of the metal boat was barely discernible as it sliced the gray waters, slowly emerging out of the fog and heading in our direction.

"The instant they're within ten feet of shore, I'll head down," I told Willy. When the boat was just about to touch the sand, I leaped from my position and slid down the eighty-degree hill— which was much slicker than I had anticipated! My noise alerted the two men in the boat whose startled, wide-eyed faces stared at the rapidly descending uniformed figure. I was caught in that panic when you know you're out of control and little can be done except hope for the best. It's amazing how much goes through your mind in an instant under these circumstances: I know for sure the end of this plummet is most likely not going to end in my favor. I see the guys whom I've pursued for so long and am actually wondering just what they might be thinking— maybe an attack by some hostile apparition. And I know that the overturned, frost-covered boat at the bottom of the hill toward which I'm accelerating is definitely not going to aid my professional approach and eventual apprehension of these culprits.

Unfortunately, I was correct in all of my adrenalin-laced predictions. I hit the boat's slick aluminum with my front foot feeling no discernible sign of grip. With that leg fighting the air and no longer a tool for deceleration, my trailing foot made brief contact but was of no use other than to assist in catapulting my entire body off the end of the overturned stern and into the air while doing an almost perfect somersault onto the newly frozen sand three feet from the bow of the target boat. Lying on my back, my first thoughts were of how pathetic an approach I had just demonstrated in order to check a license (after all, I had yet to witness a violation) and how really beautiful the wispy, sun-tinged clouds appeared while I dazedly stared up at them. Attempting to restore my professional modus operandi, I gathered up my aching bones, dusted myself off, stood at attention directly in front of the two gaping fishermen and said without any hesitation, "Wanna see that again?"

"Are you all right ?" the bowman yelled.

"Yup, just fine," I declared. "Just checking licenses and your catch this morning. Whatcha got for fish?"

I could see that they were both a little uncomfortable and silent as they dug for their licenses. By this time Willy had joined me, first complimenting me on the style of my approach and then inquiring if I could identify anything I had broken. I could see a northern pike on the back floor of the boat as we did the license inspection. A reassured feeling came over me as the illegal fish confirmed my suspicions and cemented the bargain I had with my informant. Further inspection revealed more game fish in their possession, a misdemeanor violation. Both of

Fish illegally gill-netted by a local lakeshore owner.

the violators remained quite silent during the remainder of the investigation, only remarking how startled they were.

A later look inside this person's residence indicated the love for hunting and fishing that he embraced. His entire central living area was decorated with mounted species from all over the world. Why he chose to poach his own lake was still a mystery. Sometimes the greed factor is seductive even to those who otherwise are pretty good citizens and wouldn't stand for the abuse of other laws. Hopefully, we had changed his attitude and ensured that there would be more northern pike available for all sportsmen in the south arm of Lake Pokegama.

EIGHTEEN
The Beep-Beep Blunder

The following story was submitted by retired Minnesota Department of Natural Resources (DNR) Wildlife Biologist Bill Berg who states that working with DNR Conservation Officers was always enjoyable.

Trapping furbearers has been around ever since Native Americans set foot on what is now Minnesota. But once the Voyageurs arrived, there was intense trapping pressure put on furbearers to satisfy the European fur craze. Some furbearer species, such as the very common beaver, were nearly eliminated. Further pressure was placed on furbearers when European settlers arrived. Finally in the 1920s Minnesota enacted the first regulations on trapping furbearers.

But even then there was the outlaw element that continued to harvest furbearers out of season and beyond the limit. Early game wardens and refuge patrolmen often stayed in remote outpost cabins to make it easier to catch violators. Even today, while most trappers abide by the law, illegal trapping persists in Minnesota. Some illegal trappers just take an extra animal or two or start the season a couple days early, but others are big time operators with no respect for the resource or their fellow trappers. In the late 1970s conservation officers (called game wardens before 1967) and trappers noted a sharp increase in untended and untagged traps and snares across the northern one-half of the state. This increase in suspected illegal activity coincided with high fur prices and with the 1977 fisher season, the first since 1928. Often, fisher, fox, bobcat, coyote, and pine marten (which were illegal to trap until 1985) were left to suffer for days in untended traps and snares, being left to die by unscrupulous individuals. Conservation officers sometimes camped by illegal traps with animals in them, but this time-consuming activity got old and cold and seldom resulted in the arrest of the outlaws.

Finally a conservation officer approached a DNR wildlife biologist about placing a small radio transmitter inside a dead animal in a trap. Theoretically, when the animal was removed from the trap, the radio signal would lead to the trapper's home. One cold winter night, the officer did just that and waited until the animal was taken. A few days later, an overjoyed conservation officer reported that the animal with the transmitter was gone and that a flight should be scheduled to find it. But unfortunately, the officer had not recorded the transmitter's radio frequency, so a flight was futile. Beep-beep, no beep.

But the officer had more transmitters and was instructed to record the frequency of the next transmitter and to try again. A couple days later he called again, stating that a fisher with the implanted transmitter was removed from the trap. And this time, he had recorded the frequency! An aerial search was scheduled for the next morning. Bright and early, shortly after the plane left the Grand Rapids airport, the signal was heard. After a few turns, the biologist determined that the transmitter and, hopefully, the illegal fisher were located in a house just north of U.S. Highway 2. In order to obtain a search warrant, however, one needed to have proof that the transmitter was indeed there. So two DNR biologists donned orange vests and posed as a road survey crew, walking down the road several times and waving the antenna towards the house, garage, and shed. Surely the transmitter was in one of those buildings, and the search warrant was granted.

In a short time, several conservation officers, sheriff's deputies, and wildlife biologists in multiple vehicles descended upon the property and delivered the search warrant. The elderly couple who met everyone at the door seemed a bit confused by it all and kindly let the officers in. They denied any knowledge of any illegal trapping activity, but every officer present had heard those denials before. And besides, this couple had a police scanner—standard equipment for many criminals—in their bedroom. The sound of the transmitter beeping into the biologist's headphones was proof the illegal fisher was in the house, garage, or shed. And after a few minutes of searching the premises, the signal was isolated to the bedroom, not an uncommon place for outlaws to store illegal fur.

But there was no illegal fisher or DNR transmitter or fur outlaw. Rather, the biologist's antenna pointed to the scanner on the couple's dresser, which was emitting the same radio frequency as the one in the illegal fisher. It turned out that this particular model of Bearcat scanner sometimes transmitted a radio signal! Red-faced, the officers apologized to the confused couple, accepted their invitation of coffee, and, embarrassed, went on their way. Beep-beep, wrong beep.

Early the next day, the officer and biologist took to the air again and flew by the house with the Bearcat scanner. There was no signal, and the couple likely had unplugged it. But as the plane climbed a bit higher, another signal was heard farther north and east, and after locating the signal, landing and verifying that they had the right signal this time, a search warrant was obtained and served. This time, there was no Bearcat scanner but rather, several piles of illegal animals (one with the transmitter still inside and beeping) and furs with a value exceeding $20,000. What started as a comedy of errors turned into the biggest illegal fur bust in state history! Beep-beep, right beep! Finally!

NINETEEN
The Perch Pursuit

Prior to the 1980s, the humble perch was a fish species that attained little respect among most fishermen, especially the locals. Thought of as nothing more than a forage fish for the more preferred walleyes and northern pike, the yellow perch sat near the bottom of the consumption list. This culture persisted, and until the last 25 years the perch was considered more of a nuisance that interfered with the catching of "quality" fish. The fate of many perch was reduced to the bashing of their little heads on the boat gunwales and being left for seagull and eagle fodder. The change in reputation started to come about when groups of nonresident anglers appeared on the larger walleye lakes and could be seen leaving the state with huge quantities of the tasty little delicacy. After all, if you're looking for something to fill the plate, the perch is at least as appetizing as a walleye, and through 1978, they could be taken in unlimited quantities. In 1979 they were assigned game-fish status, and the possession limit was reduced to 100 perch. This automatically enhanced its status and eventually even the local fishermen started to value the appeal of catching and eating such an easily caught and abundant fish.

Of course, the higher ranking produced more demand and not surprisingly the nonresident sportsmen began to arrive in increasing numbers, especially from eastern Wisconsin. It seems that the commercial fishing of perch allowed on Lake Michigan so drastically reduced their size and numbers that commercial taking was banned and sport fishing of perch became almost nonexistent. The problem was that these fish helped support a small industry among bars and restaurants in that part of the state where traditional Friday night fish fries consisted of perch fillets. With the supply dried up on Lake Michigan, the next most productive area was northern Minnesota, 400 miles to the west, specifically lakes Leech and Winnibigoshish. Would folks drive that far for a two-or-three day fishing trip . . . for perch? You bet they would, especially if the packaged fillets could be converted to dollars back home. At $13.00 a pound a motive for potential greed had been created. Why not enjoy a Minnesota fishing excursion and pay for the trip at the same time! Most of the people arriving from out of state were law-abiding; however, those who harbored the intent to supply a fertile market back home became ruthless in their desire to poach perch.

I had seen the steady upsurge in perch fishing traffic through the '80s and well into the '90s. Out-of-state trucks and trailers would come and go through Grand Rapids on U.S. Highway 2 increasingly earlier every year.

The illegal trafficking of perch from Lake Winnie had been happening for more than a decade but increased in the early '90s until complaints started to come in from more and more concerned fishermen and some resort owners. A few arrests on over-limits had been made, but the escalation in reported abuses prompted the local officers to concentrate more heavily on direct enforcement and monitoring of these individuals. As the work and intelligence intensified, it became necessary to use undercover methods and unmarked vehicles to identify and gain access to certain groups that appeared to show signs of evasive or otherwise suspicious behavior. A neighboring officer was assigned to patrol the lake and scrutinize larger groups fishing together. Denny would watch at a distance and try to determine intent by unusual body language, rate of fishing success and movement and location of fish and coolers. Sometimes verbal contacts were made with suspects that also provided fish accumulation numbers and times and dates of departure. This method of operation proved successful immediately with dozens of arrests being logged during the first two weeks of March 1994.

Denny called me early on a Friday night and asked if I would be available for some co-surveillance the next day. He said he was watching some prime suspects whom he thought were already over the limit and were planning on fishing another day. He watched them keeping every fish and catching them at a rate of two per minute.

The next morning I joined him about five miles north of the south shore along with my personal dog Dusty. Dusty was, in my opinion, one of the better undercover tools an officer could have in his bag. A 35-pound overweight beagle with a German shepherd puppy head, lazy ears, and short, stocky legs that barely held his belly above the ground. Even the most

Warden and faithful companion patiently surveying a group of fish poachers.

hardened poachers would never have an inkling that this K-Mart mix was an unpaid, affable, fish-detecting machine who could lick and charm his way into acceptance by outlaw groups of perpetrators. Good old Dusty would swagger over to their fishing holes looking for food and affection while giving us a chance to interface with them and pop innocent questions about their fishing success.

About four miles out on the fog-shrouded ice on Lake Winnie, two pickup trucks with fishermen came into view. They appeared to be quite an amazing crew of nine anglers. Every fish was going into the buckets, and their levels of concentration were incompatible with typical fisherman just out for a day of fun. Besides, within three hours, they had caught and kept a limit of fish. Those were the facts we needed to stop and check them on their way home: a reasonable suspicion that an over-limit was in their possession. Checking them at this time would most likely be fruitless since many of the previously caught fish would be back at a cabin. We would wait for their drive home so the fish were all concentrated in one place.

About 8:00 a.m. on Sunday morning, four other officers and I, including a member of the Grand Rapids Police Department, met to set up a roadblock on a street next to the Blandin Paper Company parking lot. As we awaited a call from Denny for the poachers' time of arrival, we arranged our vehicles into position to stop and check the two approaching pickup trucks.

"They're about three blocks away, Tom!" Denny shouted. "I'll be right behind them but I won't be joining you. Good luck!"

I could now see the two trucks stuffed with fishermen approaching us from the west. As they pulled slowly up to our red flashing lights, the first truck stopped. The trailing pickup suddenly pulled around the first truck, speeded up and shot through a small opening between our vehicles and the sidewalk, accelerating right around the local squad car. The local police turned around and took off after them, taking a right onto U.S. Highway 169. Jumping in my truck, I got behind the local squad and the chase was on. I'm thinking, "This isn't supposed to happen. They're just perch. Who would turn an over-limit of fish into a pursuit and escalate the situation into a gross misdemeanor? A high speed chase with a perch fisherman. Now that doesn't happen every day."

The driver finally had second thoughts most likely due to the overwhelming noise of sirens behind him. Pulling over about a mile south, the middle-aged male driver agreed to return to the scene of the initial stop. It didn't take long to discover his reason for wanting to evade us. Packed in stacks of coolers were packages of fish—hundreds of them. There were even fish still yet to be cleaned in one cooler. It appeared they may have fished for a while just prior to leaving for home.

I suggested, "This is going to take longer to count than the time we have here. How about just a rough estimate so they can be charged, and I'll take the perch home and make an accurate count."

Most of the packages would have to be thawed so I decided to start immediately. By mid-morning I had a count of over 3,750 perch, all obviously packaged for resale. This was a big case and similar to many groups that we had randomly happened upon three days earlier. This would be a case that hopefully would provide some pretty extensive consequences and could ultimately be used as a future deterrent for other exploiters of our resource. We would surely publicize it.

We knew the following was going to happen. They all posted bail so they could return home, and later that week only two of the nine entered guilty pleas. There would be a trial on the other seven.

And quite a trial it was. A Tuesday morning was devoted to picking a six-person jury. As the jury selection progressed, to my amazement, all six of the jurors were women, the foreman of whom was an ex-classmate of mine from 30 years ago. It didn't take long to learn what types of defendants we were dealing with. The fine or jail time they might receive was less of a concern for them than their reputations back home. It appeared we had corralled many of the city fathers of their small community. By their attitudes, it became evident that saving face and returning home with their images intact were their main concerns. Of course they contested the stop. The judge quickly took care of that. Legal and acceptable! The second day each defendant testified and contested the numbers of fish. Well, it didn't take a whole lot of work to prove the totals. I ran home and gathered up all the fish in eight coolers. During my testimony, I was asked if "Deputy Dawg Dusty," the undercover perch pooch, was a state employee. I acknowledged that he was in fact an unpaid agent of the Department and had experience and knowledge in the area of fishing enforcement.

I then asked the court if I could display the total of fish in question to the jurors and the judge. I was granted this request and immediately pulled out a blue tarp, spread it on the floor in front of the jury box and started to empty all the coolers of packaged fish out onto the plastic. It had to be impressive as cooler after cooler packed with fish poured out forming a tremendous heap in front of the judge's bench. This exhibit hopefully would show the six people in charge of making a decision just how extensive this violation was. This valuable resource belonged to them too. They were public fish that had been stolen from all of us.

The jury finally retired at 5:00 p.m. My coffee hadn't gotten cold before the bailiff announced that the jury had a verdict. "Guilty as charged on all seven defendants," the foreman announced. She later said that the jurors agreed on the first vote but waited until after the refreshments were served before they announced their decision.

"We just couldn't believe the arrogant attitude of all involved," she commented. "They were bad news and I hope their type never comes back to Minnesota." Each individual was fined $1,800 and given a sentence of 90 days in jail with 85 five days suspended.

It had been a good day and then it was time to put the finishing touches on the case. Creating a further deterrent was the next step that had to be taken. The following week, a notice of conviction was sent to their hometown newspaper for all to read and hopefully for other area culprits with the same intentions to take to heart.

For your information, the seized fish all went to a local civic group and the residents of the local nursing home. They loved them!

Addendum: This case, and others like it, helped set the stage for a statewide reduction in the 100 perch limit in 2000. The daily limit is now 20 fish with 40 in possession. This decrease has helped thwart much of the intense violating and is aiding in stabilizing the perch resource.

Bags containing 3,750 perch discovered in one pickup heading out of state.

TWENTY

The Porch-Light Poachers

When the average person thinks of deer shining and the people who engage in such activities, a mental picture usually emerges of a prowling vehicle with a couple of unsavory, inebriated characters scanning the countryside in search of a field or road ditch dotted with pairs of reflective eyes, and then a gun barrel sticking out the window. This characterization certainly bears a resemblance to many of the shining incidents that I have witnessed throughout the last 30 years. The dilapidated pickup, the handheld spotlight plugged into the cigarette lighter, the decrepit firearm and its cartridges strewn all over the floorboards and finally the odor of stale alcohol from the numerous empty and semi-empty beer cans scattered throughout the interior. This portrayal of these "bandits of the night" has evolved throughout the years. However, scenarios like these are becoming less of an occurrence since the early '90s due to increased penalties, an eruption of the rural population, and the fact that this type of behavior is not as socially condoned as it once was. Stereotypes such as this are really a sort of pigeonholing all deer poachers into one destructive wildlife force bent on creating havoc throughout the country. However, many situations and the people involved don't even come close to resembling these conditions.

Bird feeders seem to have acquired a new definition in the last 25 years. Besides more birds being attracted to home feeders due to the increase in bird feeding as a hobby in recent years, the number of nonflying creatures that gravitate toward a free meal of sunflower seeds and beef suet has also increased. Besides the usual squirrels, a feeder stuffed with numerous types of seeds can pull other critters in from long distances. The black bear, which feeds more by smell than sight, will detect the scent of sunflower seeds a mile away. This is why most wildlife and enforcement folks that deal with bear complaints at residences call these devices "bear feeders." Many kinds of four-legged creatures that wander the nearby woods will eventually find their way to this easy source of food, and in some peoples' minds, suddenly become pests. The raccoon is a good example along with porcupines, fishers, skunks and rodents of all sizes and temperaments.

Another animal that is attracted throughout the year to these swinging feed troughs is the whitetail deer. Most people enjoy seeing the deer, and selling seed and deer food is now big business. I will not debate the pros or cons of this type of recreational feeding. I will say, however, that deer feeding stations and bird feeders offer the unscrupulous a means by which a deer can easily be taken illegally and with little chance of discovery. With this method, fair play—the essence of hunting—goes out the window, and greed and laziness become the driving forces.

On a cool evening a couple of weeks before deer season, I received a call from a rural acquaintance who had just witnessed his neighbor shoot a deer. Apparently the neighbor had shot the deer under his own porch light in the front yard of his house. It seemed a bird feeder was the source of attraction, and my witness friend had observed the man drag the deer out onto his lawn. "Tom, I just can't take this anymore." my friend blurted over the phone. "I think it's time I do something about this. That's why I'm calling you. I feel like I have a moral responsibility. Could you come out?"

"I'll be right there," I answered, as I grabbed for my gun belt and jacket. "Tell me what you've witnessed so far and what your neighbor is doing right now."

"Well, I heard the shot, looked out my window and saw him approaching a downed buck deer under his porch light. He dragged it out into the front lawn and appeared to be preparing to field dress it when I walked out and told him I was going to call the game warden this time."

"What do you mean THIS time?"

"Oh, I've seen him shoot a couple deer every year this way for the last six years. Like I said, I couldn't take it anymore. It's just not fair!"

"You've done the right thing by calling, but I just wish you wouldn't have told him I was coming. That may make things a little more difficult."

"That won't be a problem. He said he would just be waiting for you by the deer."

I was a little hesitant at this point to go directly to the scene without assistance, but at midnight, there was no one available, and besides, I knew the person with whom I was about to have contact! Even then, it isn't often that a deer poacher is willing to just give up and wait for the inevitable.

As I entered the dark winding driveway, I could see a faint outline of a person sitting on the lawn next to a dark mass that materialized into a deer carcass when my headlights shone across the front yard. "C'mon over here, Tom. I knew you were coming," the man responded as I came forward from my patrol vehicle. He conceded to the fact that he was caught and was basically awaiting the consequences of his illegal actions. The whole scene was a little strange, having to arrest a person for a gross misdemeanor when the guy was totally cooperative, besides being a good and well-informed citizen.

It always amazed me as to the extent poaching reaches into all levels of society. Even the most honorable members of the community are sometimes tempted by the poaching bug. I believe this was a perfect example of an illegal behavior becoming so routine that it turned habitual, even acceptable, in the person's mind.

There was one thing left in this case that was always consistent with my interrogations; I needed the weapon! Not only for evidence but to deny him of the use of this particular firearm to ever again take an illegal animal. He was a little reluctant until I made him aware of the alternative—jailing and fingerprinting. He figured he didn't need that and willingly surrendered the rifle to my possession. I left him in about as good a spirit as could be expected and wished him a good evening.

A large fine and three years of no big game hunting were awaiting him. It would be so nice if respect could go both ways in all poaching cases. This was one such case.

My neighboring officer Willy called me one fall afternoon and asked me to help him with something he had found along the road in the northern part of my patrol area. He had discovered a freshly skinned deer hide in the ditch of a county road, and it appeared to have a bullet hole through the chest area. Finding deer hides along highways isn't that uncommon because of the high numbers of deer hit by cars. Other times a person will discard deer remains along a roadway after processing the meat rather than properly disposing by burying or taking to a landfill. Very few have bullet holes, so this was definitely worth some further scrutiny. Making a case like this, if in fact the deer was taken illegally, was just about impossible. With no evidence linking the hide to anyone or anything, it normally passes as just another unsolved case of a poached deer. One should know that very few deer poaching cases are ever discovered or solved. The ones you hear about are those rare times when luck and fate happened to cross paths with a warden or when a tip call guided the officer to the culprit. This turned out to be one of those unbelievable exceptions! "Look here, Tom," Willy declared. "I think we might have something."

We had laid the hide out flat to further inspect the bullet hole, when we found stuck to the hide a blood-drenched and mutilated front page of the *Hibbing Daily Tribune*. So what might this little shred of evidence reveal? Would you believe, a subscriber label with full name and address. "I don't know if this will lead us anywhere, Willy, but if it accomplishes what I think you're hoping, you'd better frame this little piece of newsprint."

Willy was animated. "Let's make a visit," he expounded. "How about tonight?"

It didn't take long for us to find the residence in the dark. The north shoreline of Deer Lake is dotted with homes and cabins, most having distinct identification on the mail boxes. The 15-mile trip seemed a long way from where the hide was discovered. A garage was the first building along the driveway that led up to a house 100 feet up the hill. Between the house and the garage sat a four-wheeler with a rope wound around the back frame. As we walked the pathway to the house, we immediately noticed blood, not only on the rope but also on the dirt entryway in front of the garage door.

With this evidence, we hoped that a search warrant would not be necessary, of course depending on the attitude of the owner. We still could not search without one, but with the overwhelming facts of hide, blood and newspaper, we assumed that the owner would cooperate and allow a consent search.

But if we were to ever meet a character for the record books, this was the place. A knock on the door launched the next half hour into some of the worst expletives directed at two officers I've ever witnessed. The large, cantankerous guy put on the finest act of intimidation of his life. He knew he was had, but he put us in a position where we were forced to listen to his life history including his many rowdy experiences in the Merchant Marine. Actually, his stories were fascinating. I almost forgot why we were there until Willy nudged me, "I think it's time, Tom. We have to get in that garage."

So with that, the man's cussing and yelling came to a close. We showed him our evidence and made it very clear that we were not about to leave until we were satisfied that there were no illegal deer on his premises. From that moment on, the "wild thing" turned into a teddy bear. "It's in the garage," he declared in a somewhat reserved fashion. "I shot it under the bird feeder!" His matter-of-fact manner and quick turnabout had me on edge for a moment, considering what we had witnessed the last 30 minutes, until we found the skinned deer hanging inside the dark garage. Further inspection of the bird feeder on the hill outside his kitchen window showed evidence of deer blood and hair where the animal had fallen. He admitted to shooting the buck under the rays of his porch light and then attaching it to his four-wheeler and dragging it into the garage. Our poacher had now become our buddy. After the necessary paperwork, he restarted his life stories and what brought him to this fine area. Amazingly, I was starting to be impressed. He had quite a history and now he had an audience. Even under these conditions, we listened. He turned out to be an OK fella, not unlike many of the poachers with whom we deal.

As we left the scene with the deer in the back of our truck, my thoughts were absorbed by bird feeders. This was the second case in as many years where a bird feeder was a major element in the illegal taking of a big game animal. "Is this a trend?" I wondered. "Or just coincidence?" Who knows!

Addendum: As I write these stories, I was informed of a local incident that took place and was prosecuted in the last month. It seems an individual came home late in the evening somewhat intoxicated. Outside under his porch light stood a deer feeding on seed dropped from a bird feeder. With his mighty .22 caliber rifle, the man hurried to the basement, and with one impressive shot, killed the deer—by blasting through his own basement window. He then dragged the carcass to his garage for processing the next day. I understand the blood trail in the snow and the exit hole in the window were big factors in making the case. This occurred in January so apparently the time of year has no effect on "*bird-feeder poaching*."

Over-limit of 95 crappies found hidden in a sled.

Loon entangled in monofilament line caused by an illegal "set" line off a dock.

**Bald Eagle caught in snare near an illegally set bait for furbearers.
The bait wasn't covered as the law requires.
The eagle survived.**

More **POACHERS CAUGHT!**

Numerous muskrats found in traps illegally set before season.

A warden's mailbox stuffed full of illegally taken walleye remains
by an unscrupulous fish poacher.

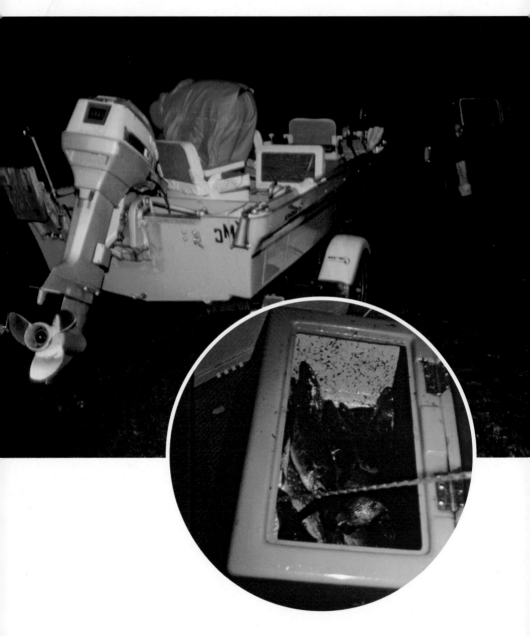

Many species of protected fish discovered in live-well
two weeks before season.

**Cooler containing an over-limit of 185 walleyes discovered
in trunk of a fish poacher's car.**

Three protected Timber Wolves found illegally snared over one night.

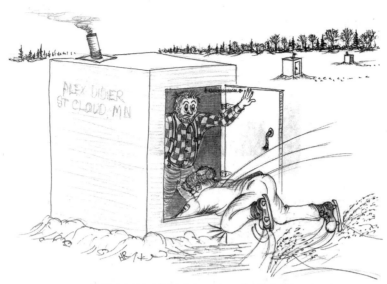

TWENTY ONE
The Fishy Tales

It's hard to persevere in a game warden career without some pretty funny things going down. A humorous episode is more often than not right around the corner; it's that singular ingredient that helps maintain the fascination and appeal of the job. Finally, humor preserves the special memories accumulated over time. Typically, the tales told first are the ones that in the end have elicited the most laughter. I suppose that's true in most professions, but game wardening is unique in that it deals with people who are caught up in circumstances beyond their control, due many times to their own flawed decision-making. When a human is captured in the act of committing a no-no while assuming that there was zilch chance of being observed, sometimes irrational comments and behaviors transpire at the scene. Much of the bizarre conduct is also triggered by the realization of imminent punishment—perhaps the possibility of jail, stiff fines or sudden, uninvited notoriety.

A particularly noteworthy event had to do with opening fishing day on Lake Winnibigoshish. I remember the day as cool and windy with fishing boats scrunched into groups on the north shore. This portion of the lake afforded some relief from the escalating winds that morning, but the blustery weather didn't dampen the fishing success. I was working under the direction of my partner who had experienced this scene many times. His approach was to employ covert means in order to apprehend the wily walleye villains, many of whom were taking and keeping fish well beyond their legal limit. Each with a companion, we cast off in separate boats toward the swarm of activity. The fish appeared to be biting feverishly as we kept the boats under observation, occasionally casting a line for added cover. As we drifted up close to fishermen, we would check their licenses and catches while remaining barely detectable.

After inspecting about 50 boats, we met up with Willy about 10:00 a.m. "How'd you guys do? Any major infractions so far?" I inquired.

"We've had quite an interesting morning. Tie up with us. We'll show you what we've got."

Glancing at the floor of his boat, I could see a stringer of walleyes. "What did you do, find an over-limit already?"

"Actually, they found us," Willy gloated back. "A boat just approached us and asked if we wanted some fish. I said, 'Sure, why not? How many you got?' Well, they proceeded to tell us that they were way over-limit on fish already and wondered if we could take their extras so they could continue fishing. 'Don't want to get caught by the wardens with too many.' So we accommodated them; we took their fish … and all the others too." How's that for the good luck/bad luck syndrome?

I'm thinking, "Of the hundreds of boats out here, they pick an undercover warden boat. Now that's beyond statistical explanation. It's just dreadfully bad luck." It was a good laugh on our end, but I can only imagine what transpired back at camp for those boys that morning.

Many comical moments revolved around fishing and people trying their darndest to acquire them by illegal means. It just so happened a couple of laughable confrontations took place on the same creek.

For less than ten days each year, a well-known little stream south of Grand Rapids was home to hundreds of spring-spawning northern pike. It was visited by many of the local residents who counted on a preseason meal or two of fresh fish, picked from the cold, shallow water after dark. Some of these would-be poachers were young, and to say the least, amateurish in their approach. Many of the neighboring officers liked to work this spot because, for some strange reason, the word on our warden presence had yet to be broadcast. It was easy pickings since there was basically only one place to grab a fish—the infamous culvert. The scoundrels would advance toward this small drain from all directions, usually well after dark. I suppose they assumed the warden service called it a day when the clock struck midnight and that the fun could begin.

One cool early morning, my partner and I were set up across the road from the drainage so as to view any questionable activities. About half the intruders would arrive on foot, others by vehicle. This particular night I had the distinct advantage of a night-scope in my toolbox. This little device would allow complete, "daylight" observation of the entire area, including creeping humans. Earlier that evening, we had detained a couple of juveniles who showed up with spears, another device not allowed near a creek at that time of year. The spears were seized, and Mom and Dad would be contacted the next morning about their kids' treachery.

About 1:00 a.m., a pickup truck pulled up next to the culvert and shut its lights off. The less light, the more I could see with my secret weapon. Immediately, the lone male driver had a grip on a large, wriggling, slippery pike. As the fish thief crossed the road with northern in hand, the squirmy thing escaped from his clutch and hit the center of the blacktop with a loud "splat." He gathered up the fish and ran it to the base of a white pine tree about 20 feet off the opposite side of the roadway. I could hear the pike thrashing while the guy went back for another. His source of light was only a small penlight, almost invisible, even through my night-vision appliance. Across the road he ran, again clasping another large northern pike. Large pike were somewhat rare in this creek, but this fella knew his trade; he had performed this ritual before. Now on his third and final trip across the road to the pine, the sneaky pilferer was constantly glancing in both directions for any approaching vehicle lights, totally unaware that he was as visible as if he were darting around in the middle of the afternoon.

We'd seen enough and were now ready to take enforcement action. "We'll grab him when he puts the fish in the truck," I whispered to my partner.

As we shifted into a ready position, the unexpected happened—our preseason fisherman jumped in his truck and took off, without the fish. "Wow. This guy HAS done this before. He'll be back later when he's sure the coast is clear," I deliberated, as we inspected the hidden booty. "Three nice pike, the largest about ten pounds. He'll definitely be back. We'll just wait."

An hour later, our prognosis was correct. Up rattled the little truck. It turned around and was left idling as the three pike were retrieved and placed in the box. We were now sitting motionless in our darkened truck taking notes on the whole operation. He started east, with us right behind him. "Traveling black," we stayed behind using his taillights as guidance. "Let's just follow him home or wherever he's going," I said. "It'll be safer, and who knows what we'll find there?"

We tagged along behind for more than five miles until the truck turned into a driveway. We were forced to stay clear until he exited the truck for fear of him driving off. As soon as the lights came on in the residence, we pulled in and inspected the truck. The fish had already been removed, so we walked up to the door. We were greeted by a relatively young man with no shirt who was obviously feigning sleepiness.

"Whatda you guys want?" he stated in an innocent manner.

"Game wardens! We need to talk to you about the fish you just snatched from the creek down the road. Have anything to say about that?"

"I know nothing about any fish. Why don't you guys just leave me alone."

"Speaking of alone. Are you alone here?"

"Yup," he admitted with an unyielding attitude in his voice.

"Well, we know exactly what you were up to. To convince you of our proof, why don't you take a look through this?" as I handed him the night vision scope. "Just take a look through the lens here. What do you think?"

As he pointed the device outside into the blackness, his only reaction was, "WOW!

From then on his denial had little substance other than to tell us we were probably going to court on this one. This fella wasn't the type to admit anything. And just as I thought, a month later we were all sitting in front of a judge who listened intently to the testimony. I prefer a trial by judge, and this case was a good example why. The judge had little sympathy for the defendant's denials of what took place that night. "Guilty as charged" was his immediate finding. Most violators learn something positive from an experience such as this and are deterred from future illicit behavior. I believe this was an exception.

Same creek, different night. Another partner and I had the culvert area under surveillance from our same hideout. This time two shadowy figures appeared moving around the channel area. Without the help of night vision (I had given the scope to another officer), we had to keenly observe with the limited light and listen intently for signs of fish removal. As the minutes wore on, a fish could finally be seen in the light from their flashlights. Apparently they had walked a distance from a parked vehicle and were about to carry some fish back to their car. "Might as well take them now," I quietly declared to my fellow officer. "Game wardens! Hold it right there!" we both shouted. That's all it took. Both of our targets made tracks in separate directions, one running back across the ditch bank, the other gathering speed eastbound down the center of the road into the darkness—with me on his tail. The first thing to hit the ground was a fish that squirted from the culprit's tense grip. Hurdling over the pike, I concluded the 50-yard dash with a final lunge at the feet of the sprinting escapee. In an instant, we were both flat on our stomachs hugging the cold asphalt. Clutching his leg, I shifted to a more manageable position. "OK, let's both stand up and just relax," I instructed. "First thing, I need is some identification, like your name."

"My name's Chapin," he said in a submissive tone.

"It's not exactly the right moment to be witty. I need to know who you are."

"Really, sir. Chapin's my name. I'm the other one."

"What the heck are you doing out here, Chapin? Not your best choice was it?"

"Yeah, I know," the young man replied. "Just thought we'd have some fun. Remember the 6-foot rabbit call?"

"As a matter of fact I do," I answered, as we strolled back to the culvert.

"I imagine you've gotten lots of strange calls, he offered."

"Yeah, all the time, but that was the most memorable."

A couple of years ago, a friend of mine from the Twin Cities instigated a hoax by explaining that he had a 6-foot rabbit in his front yard and asking if I could come and get it. The problem was that he called the wrong Chapin . . . the other Chapin.

After we met with my partner and his runaway, a pretty good laugh was had by all. This was a good family, and we reminisced about the association of our matching name in regards to my job. His final declaration: "Boy, you sure get a lot of calls!"

I've reiterated how the spring fish run was the most exciting of times in this line of work, at least as far as I'm concerned.

"Wild" and "extreme" don't do justice to some of the crazy incidents witnessed during the weeks prior to the opening of fishing season.

One that comes to mind developed as I was investigating a possible gill-netting violation in the Trout Lake area. I finally fingered the character involved but was stymied as to his exact whereabouts. I feverishly worked all day on the information provided me, hoping that the evidence would still be accessible. It was close to sunset, and my prospects of finding either the fish or the perpetrator were deteriorating fast.

There was one final option at my disposal—the girlfriend. I was saving this for my last resort. The likelihood of his female companion having knowledge of out-of-season fish was slim but definitely worth a final shot.

I learned the location of the upstairs apartment by inquiring with the local police department in the small town. My brows raised as I was informed of previous police visits to this same address regarding suspected infractions. "Maybe there's still a chance," I muttered to myself as I climbed the steep outside stairs to the second floor. Lacking probable cause, I knew it was necessary to get permission to search or I would have to walk away with nothing. I wasn't even quite sure of what I was look-ing for other than "some fish."

Numbers and species were not included in the original tip.

As soon as the young lady answered the door, I perceived something amiss. As I made my identity known, her uneasy body language and edgy manner of speech revealed a lot. She knew something, and it was my job to gain her confidence.

"I'm here to investigate the taking and possible possession of illegal fish that may have been netted by your boyfriend. Could you help me out here? I'm really busy tonight and I need your cooperation. Anything you could assist me with would be appreciated. I'm sure you aren't involved, so I wonder if you could let me take a quick look in your freezer and I'll be outa here. Of course, I would only look with your permission."

I gave her all the options at once and waited for her reac-tion. I was astounded when she answered with a whimpered,

"Sure, I guess it's alright. I think I know what you're looking for, anyway."

As I entered the kitchen area, she walked into the adjoining bathroom and said, "I guess this is what you want," pointing in the direction of the bathtub.

Well, I had never seen anything like it thus far in my young career. There they were. A dozen northern pike, some real hogs, swimming in unison around the inside edge of a full tub of bathwater. I can't say I've ever thought of storing fish in my personal bathtub, but this was a different situation. Having to go to work immediately following his early morning gill-netting scheme, the poacher knew it was critical to keep the fish alive to prevent spoiling prior to processing—and where else but in his own private tub.

Now it was time to "pull the plug" on this operation—literally. I would be putting a "drain" on their resources, a "sinking" feeling, but that was my job; to carry out my duties as a sworn agent for the State. The "scales" of justice swirled our way.

There comes a time in a person's career when one has to ride above an embarrassing situation and just accept the inevitable—even with your badge shined and your uniform starched, you *will* be laughed at!

As I patrolled Lake Winnibigoshish one sunny afternoon, I pulled my boat alongside a single fisherman who I noticed was fishing with an extra line. He was a congenial individual, and we began to talk about mutual friends and places. There was no ill feeling about the summons I was about to issue, and our chatter during the next 20 minutes was interesting and pleasant.

I did, however, start to recognize symptoms of boating stress: a slight headache most likely caused by extended exposure to the hot sun and blurred vision that was becoming more evident as I attempted to write the ticket. In fact, it was so difficult to see the numbers and letters that I made a decision to call it a day after this contact. I wore corrective lens sunglasses, but they seemed to be of little use during this episode.

After wishing the fellow a good day, I turned the boat and headed for the access, eight miles away. I was continuing to experience unusual, blurred eyesight as I reached up and adjusted my dark glasses. There was a lens missing. The left glass had obviously popped out, and I had been operating with one restricted and one dilated pupil simultaneously the last half hour. No wonder things appeared totally out of whack. "What exactly was going through the mind of the two-liner," I instantly wondered. There he was, sitting and politely conversing with me the whole time, while I stared back at him with one eye visible. I couldn't believe he didn't mention something about my cyclopean appearance or the peculiar fashion of my eyewear. Nope! He just figured, why bother. He was getting a ticket and it wasn't his job to be critical of the man in charge. I imagine he had a good laugh at my expense with his buddies.

It's a bit unusual for ice conditions at freeze-up to be smooth and snow-free. Normal years find jagged chunks of wind-blown ice covering the entirety of Lake Pokegama.

This particular year, it was just the opposite. First freeze had formed a perfectly smooth icescape as the result of windless, cold conditions the previous night. The following day, fishermen were pulling their fish shelters out on the 4-inch-thick ice and preparing for the next day's opening of northern pike spearing season. Dark house spearing is such a ritual in the area that most fishermen assume that, barring open water, they will be out there December 1 no matter what the conditions.

This was an exceptional and rare opener, and I decided that checking fish shelters on ice skates could be the technique of the day. Why not just skate up to the unsuspecting fishermen and check for violations and fishing success? What a thrill to soar along, especially in the shallower water, and observe schools of fish darting in all directions under your feet. I chose to move downwind across Pokegama Lake that day to gather speed and check more houses in less time. I assumed I would be panting on my 10 mile trip back, but the uniqueness of the situation was worth the effort.

As I stopped to inspect house after house, I was surprised how much I could accomplish in so little time. Besides, not one person was aware of my approach until my knock on the door. Just this small advantage yielded a half a dozen minor violations but also made a positive impression on the legal folks who thought my enforcement style to be very upbeat. I noticed the wind really picking up, so I was forced to pay particular attention to my approaching glide rate.

That's when it happened. I should have known that a quick stop on this smooth, wind-glossed surface was becoming more difficult. Just as I skated high-speed and downwind straight toward an unwary fisherman's door, it opened! And in I went, directly into the shelter, no time for the usual, "How's fishing . . . like to check your license" approach. I crumpled against the opposite wall and found myself looking down into the open spear hole with my skates wrapped around the spear rope. The occupant had been stepping outside just as I whizzed by him and was still staring as I picked myself up as professionally as I could under the conditions. "Sorry about that," I said as I stepped back outside. "That's the first time I've checked a house from the inside out. Hope I didn't hurt anything here. Still have to check your license, though."

Remarkably, the middle-aged man was incredibly understanding and seemed to be genuinely concerned about my well-being. I wished him well, skated off to the next house . . . and of course modified my angle of attack.

One example of illegally speared spring walleyes, all 4–13 pounds.

TWENTY TWO
The Webbed Tales

igratory waterfowl enforcement has always been a high priority for game wardens in the fall of each year. The bear and upland game seasons are already in full swing by the time the duck and goose seasons kick off in late September and early October. By federal definition, migratory waterfowl are ducks (including mergansers) and geese. Regulations involving the methods of taking, limits, and possession are a combination of state and federal laws, both of which are enforced by state officers. A violation of the migratory bird laws can result in a trip to federal court in some instances.

Duck populations in general have been deteriorating for decades throughout the country, mostly due to habitat loss in the northern tier of states and in Canada's prairie pothole regions. Waterfowl hunting has always been a major sporting tradition, and much pressure is put on the governmental units in charge to provide regulations to sustain this institution even as the duck populations continue to dwindle. This is why enforcement is such an important factor in the future of this popular hunting activity.

Although located on the eastern edge of the central water-fowl migration route, some areas of Itasca County have traditionally attracted large numbers of ducks, particularly in the west and northwest sectors. The Mississippi backwaters, Lake Winnibigoshish and Bowstring and Squaw lakes are good examples of large water expanses known for some of the better waterfowl hunting in the area. The following accounts are just a few examples of illegal (and goofy) behavior that I've witnessed while checking duck hunters in these areas.

One particular occurrence involving duck hunters happened on one of the many small lakes in my patrol area where the habitat was favorable to both ducks and fish. Although the fishing was only fair, the residents knew it as a home for locally reared mallards as well as an attraction for the first migrants of the year including teal and wood ducks.

It was just after dawn on the third day of duck season as I positioned myself in the rear seat of the canoe. My friend in the bow pushed us off with his paddle into the thin layer of fog that shrouded most of the lake. I seldom used a motor on the square-stern craft, but this particular lake had more shoreline than I could cover by paddling. Besides, we weren't even sure there was any hunting activity, so the entire trip around the lake could be for naught.

The little 4-horse outboard putted us steadily along the bulrush and cattail shoreline while we looked and listened for any movement or shots in the distance. About a half hour into our tour, the sun had risen above the trees, transforming the surface of the water into a shimmering pool of diamond-like reflections. We were already halfway around the perimeter of the lake with no sign of human disturbance. An occasional mallard quack and a couple of small flocks of wood ducks whistling overhead were the only sounds in the crisp morning air. "One more point of land to work around and we can get out of here," I declared to my partner. "Our next lake will have hunters. I guarantee it!"

Just as we rounded the peninsula, a boat appeared about 300 yards down the shoreline. The image through my binoculars showed two people, rods in hand, trolling for fish along the edge of the jutting weed-bed. "Looks like a couple of fishermen. Might as well check them on the way back to our truck."

The person in the bow of their small boat was the first to spot our rear approach. Being only 200 feet behind them, I could see the bowman signal our presence to his motorman. The operator then looked back in our direction as we glided within 50 feet of their stern. As I motioned for him to slow to a stop, his head immediately snapped into a forward position, and his little 5-horse Evinrude was suddenly under full power. "Hold up a minute!" I shouted. "Game Warden. We just want to check you guys out."

The hollering and gesturing was to no avail as we skimmed along behind them as fast as our tiny 4-horse would push us. "What the heck are these guys up to?" I wondered.

Then I realized I was in pursuit of a 5-horsepowered fishing boat. And what was more unsettling, I wasn't quite sure I was ever going to catch them! Then I thought, "Where can they go? This isn't like a highway. We're on a big bowl of water."

The speeds on the straight stretches exceeded 12 miles per hour at times with no appreciable reduction in our gap. As the wind blew by our tear-swollen eyes, I suddenly recognized the driver. An easily recognizable individual of tall, slim stature, this guy was one of the most mild-mannered people you could find. Again, "What the heck is going on here?" I pondered. Then I noticed an almost imperceptible gain on our pursuees. Foot-by-foot, yard-by-yard, we were creeping forward along their wake. Within a minute, our canoe was bouncing alongside their straining aluminum boat, and that was when I saw it—the reason this whole scene turned into a chase fiasco—an uncased shotgun lying on the floor of their boat. They were shooting ducks and trolling for northern pike . . . at the same time! (Transporting any uncased and/or loaded firearm in any type of motorized vehicle is illegal.)

I certainly didn't think this little infraction was worthy of an outboard breakaway, but they apparently didn't see it that way. "C'mon boys, slow it down. It's not worth the gas," I shouted. I could hear their throttle back off and watched as their boat slowed to a stop alongside our gunwale. The driver, with a sheepish look, handed me the shotgun and said, "Just thought we'd try for a few ducks while pike fishing. Figured we could get the gun cased before you stopped us. That's about it!"

As we sat and discussed the situation, a female mallard squawked overhead as she set her wings for a landing in the nearby wild rice bed. "Guess you'll have to decide which it's going to be today," I said. "Hunting or fishing."

"I think we'll stick to the fishing for now, Tom," the driver muttered with a slight smile directed my way.

It was always a pleasure to have help from other officers during the annual duck seasons. Occasionally, Dave, A federal game warden from Duluth and an employee of the U.S. Fish and Wildlife Service, would work with me on a weekend. Not only did I learn a great deal about waterfowl enforcement during his visits, but also we accumulated quite a number of memorable incidents while working together over the years.

The first time we combined forces involved a local taxidermist. Dave had been doing some undercover work prior to informing me about this person. After enough evidence had been accumulated, Dave then contacted me for assistance in bringing the case to conclusion.

The business of taxidermy is an occupation that is closely monitored by both the Department of Natural Resources and the U.S. Fish and Wildlife Service. The majority of taxidermists are talented professionals who adhere to the rules and regulations. Requirements include the keeping of sales and mounting records of each protected species and maintaining an inventory list of animals in possession, each tagged with the owner's identification. The reason for this trail of paperwork is to ensure that the businesses are mounting only those animals that can legally be possessed and that the proper permits are in place.

Sometimes the pressure by a client to mount an "illegal species" such as a hawk, owl, eagle, songbird or even a timber wolf is financially overwhelming, and the taxidermist will succumb to that predominant driving force in almost all wildlife violations—greed!

Dave's local suspect was just one of these. I had been suspicious of this fellow even before Dave's attention, so I was looking forward to seeing what type of evidence Dave had amassed. I learned what we would be looking for when a search warrant to inspect the man's residence was granted.

Taxidermy is hard work and very time consuming. It appeared that this individual was spending the bulk of his time on mounting and selling illegal ducks, songbirds, cub bears and fish. Our search took us to three freezers in the garage, each of which was filled with ducks and birds of all varieties. Ducks are not illegal to have in possession but only with proper paperwork and proof that they were taken legally. These ducks didn't fill that requirement. All 45-five ducks found frozen or in various stages of mounting were "spring ducks." This means each duck was shot in the spring out of season—we later found out along the Mississippi River west of town—for the sole purpose of resale. Spring ducks have much brighter plumage than ducks taken in the fall and can garner high prices from those unscrupulous enough to want something like this to hang on their walls or display on their mantles. Also, federal law bans the sale of any migratory waterfowl, even mounted specimens.

Next came the bears. Three 30-pound bear cub hides ready for mounting were found in another freezer. Cub bears have been illegal to possess in Minnesota since the mid-'60s. We assumed these were shot out of trees in the early fall while their mother was trying to protect them. I believe these also would have brought a hefty price, but I always wondered who would have the nerve to display them.

Finally, besides the numerous hawks, owls and colorful songbirds were the largemouth bass. I had never seen bass that big because Minnesota doesn't have bass that big. A box of frozen bass, all 9 to 13 pounds, was found nestled in the bottom of the third freezer. They had been imported from Florida, where bass grow to this size, and were ready to be mounted for some local sportsmen. This whole arrangement is a violation of the federal Black Bass Act which prohibits the sale and illegal trafficking of bass.

Charges were brought resulting in a six-month jail term, a large fine and a complete firearm possession restriction for five years.

Dave and I had two incidents in the same day that we still talk about. Early one morning on the second weekend of duck season, we noticed an older gentleman in a duck boat pulled off in the reeds along the west bank of the Mississippi River. He appeared to be calling it quits for the day and began motoring up the shoreline toward his personal boat access near his residence. We let him disembark before landing behind him. "Hello, sir, couple of game wardens. Like to check your bag and licenses," Dave declared.

It seemed odd immediately that there was no response. He was either deaf or wanted nothing to do with us as he kept a steady pace up the bank toward his house. Dave got out first and walked up next to the guy repeating who we were and what we wanted, but again, no response. I helped Dave restrain the man by each of us holding his jacket and physically stopping him. The facial expression said it all. He wanted nothing to do with us. After we asked for his license and migratory bird stamps, he slowly and deliberately removed his license from his wallet, and, still without a word, and threw them on the ground.

Other than his strange and unfriendly behavior, the man had complied with our orders until Dave asked him to sign his federal duck stamp. It's a violation to hunt without signing your name across the face of the stamp, but the majority of the time, officers will give a break and allow the hunter to sign it in front of them.

The first words we heard from this gentleman were, "I'm not signing that (blankety-blank) thing, and there's nothing you can do about it."

"Well, at least the guy can speak," I thought. "What's next? I mean, we're giving the guy a break, and he's fighting us about a simple signature."

Dave had more patience than I did through the next 15 minutes of tirades and temper tantrums. The gentleman became so aggressive that we thought we might have to cuff him . . . over a duck stamp. When he started to throw things, I thought it time to just let him go, issue a summons and leave. That's just what we did, only Dave issued the summons—for federal court, for failure to comply with the migratory waterfowl rules by not signing a federal duck stamp.

This case wouldn't have been so memorable but for the fact that the gentleman pled "not guilty" and had to make a trip to appear in front of a federal magistrate in Minneapolis, Minnesota. Of course, Dave had to make the same trip, only to witness the final frustration. After all this, the judge allowed the man to sign the stamp in front of him and found him not guilty! How's that for justice!

Later that morning, Dave and I were motoring down the winding, open channel on the west bank through the wild rice when two shots to our left got our attention. "Look at that guy in the rice," I hollered at Dave. "He's shooting ducks from his motorboat. Let's see if we can check him."

Dave was in the front of my boat and got the man's attention by signaling with a handheld stop sign and shouting for him to stop. Dave also produced a badge to identify our intentions. It took no time at all to see that our illegal duck shooter had no intention of stopping.

We could see the shotgun on the seat and pulled within 20 feet of him before our prop was overcome with rice stalks. Twenty feet! I felt like a hefty toss of our anchor could have just about reached, but here we were, stuck in the rice. Of course, so was he! As Dave watched the hunter remove the rice from his motor, I hurriedly tipped our motor up and removed the thick gobs that entangled the prop. "Hurry up," Dave hollered. "He's getting away."

"OK. Now we've got him," I shouted. "We're right on his tail." The problem was the wild rice was so thick that neither of us could make any progress. As soon as we became bogged down, so did he. This whole chase was going to come down to who was the quickest rice remover. Dave started to paddle from the bow, but I wasn't doing too well. Because of the weight of both Dave and I in our boat, it was hard to compete with our single perpetrator. He could go slightly farther every time we had to de-rice.

This adrenalin-filled rice-bed chase went on for another fifteen minutes before I realized we weren't going to catch this guy. He was closing in on the open channel, and once he hit that, it was smooth sailing and goodbye wardens. My prediction was right. There sat Dave and I, 10 feet from open water, watching our violator throttle his way out of sight. "Whatdaya say, Dave. Want to give chase?"

The look on Dave's sweating face and his deep, gasping breaths said everything. "Let's go get a hamburger!

This next case is one that should disgust not only every sportsman but also anyone who has a clear understanding of the responsibilities that come with harvesting our resources. I describe this case to make a strong point not only to the hunting public but also to those nonhunters and folks who have a hard time justifying hunting. I guarantee you, the vast majority of hunters find wanton waste of animals deplorable and would be the first to condemn this type of behavior.

It began with a call from a local police officer about some ducks he had seen hanging from a clothesline in the backyard of a local residence. Apparently, a hunter or hunters had strung up a large number of scaup and ring-neck ducks along four strands of clothesline and had left them there for a long time. Upon inspection, they appeared to have not been field dressed and were hanging with their beaks up.

I would have gone straight to the residence and interviewed the owner, but the ducks already appeared to be spoiled, and it would be easier to charge the individual if there was conclusive evidence that he intended to destroy them. I decided to wait until they were physically removed and thrown away.

It was a long wait. November, December, January, February passed with no change in the hanging duck setting! With help from my police friend, it was a daily trip past the house.

Finally, in March, my friend called me early one morning and told me they were gone; the ducks were no longer hanging in the yard as they had been the last four months. I immediately called the sanitation department to check on their pickup dates. The next day was scheduled for a garbage pickup at the residence. I checked with the County Attorney's office as to my

Unprocessed ducks found thrown in the garbage can, an example of wanton waste.

limits for searching a garbage can. I was told that once the garbage was placed in the truck, it was then open for inspection.

The next morning, I was there. I inspected and found what I was looking for, 22 ducks, all spoiled. The law is clear here. A person must either consume or give away all legally acquired game and fish.

It's not necessary to describe the particular fellow involved. He went to court and paid his fine—$250. Hopefully, he learned something.

This final example shows how humor is many times interwoven into an otherwise routine check.

It was a dark and dreary November morning, the light cold drizzle making every attempt to develop into snow flurries. In other words, perfect conditions for a sunrise shoot of migrating northern scaup. It takes a good-size lake to attract these diver ducks . . . and it takes real die-hard hunters to be out there shooting at them.

I knew that Trout Lake was a perfect spot for these late season ducks to rest and feed on their way south. Large migrations of these birds would only fly for three or four days, so hopefully this gray, overcast morning would attract some local hunting activity.

My suspicions panned out immediately as I drove into the access area. Scanning the vegetation along the east shore through my spotting scope, I quickly picked up the image of two hunters a mile away having a good shoot. Several shots echoed each time a flock of ducks came into their decoy set. As I strained to see through the foggy mist, I observed that the hunters were also darn good marksmen. Seeing three ducks drop in one flurry of shots within five minutes of observation convinced me to wait them out.

Within a half hour and four more dead ducks, the two picked up their decoys and motored in my direction—directly to the access. This would just be a typical duck inspection: licenses, plugs and limit checks.

"Looks like you got some great shooting out there," I said, as they pulled their boat onto the sandy shore. "What a great morning for divers. It appears you've done pretty good."

"Yeah, great, Tom. I believe we got our limit."

"Well, let's see what you've got while you get your licenses out."

The one fellow was wearing a trench-type rain suit and seemed to be holding his lower arms and elbows close to his body as he struggled to remove his wallet from his back pocket. My count put them on the legal limit of four ducks apiece, which raised my suspicion due to my witnessing the earlier shooting. "Are these all the ducks you've got?"

"You're lookin at them, Tom. We missed a lot."

"Are you sure? I know you as a pretty good shot."

"What you see is what we've got," he reiterated.

As we stood facing each other, I continued my small talk, unconvinced of their sincerity. The longer we stood eye-to-eye, the more fidgety he got—until PLOP . . . PLOP . . . PLOP—three more ducks dropped from under his jacket onto his feet. I looked down, glanced back at his slightly grinning face and asked him if he had more in his pockets. "Nope. That's about it, Tom. I told you, we missed more than we hit!"

A person of good humor, the hunter began to laugh at his situation and yielded to my enforcement actions. "What the heck. I had to try it. They were just flying too good! This is the first time I've ever been busted, Tom," he proclaimed.

"Hopefully this will help you think next time 'They're flying too good,'" I replied, as I handed him the summons.

TWENTY THREE
The Case for Melvin

T he following true account was written by Minnesota
State Conservation Officer Dennis Lang. I chose this
story as an example of the rehabilitation process that
can begin when a poacher finally comes to terms with his own
behavior. It also demonstrates what can happen when an officer
pays attention to the "human element" of his or her work.

Game wardens, or conservation officers as they are now
referred to, are fortunate to spend a lot of time out of doors and
enjoy some of the best experiences the natural world offers.
After spending 16 years in one station known for its lakes,
woods and public land, I needed a change. I accepted a transfer
to another station in west-central Minnesota known for its large
numbers of lakes and quality fishing and hunting.

Not long after arriving at my new station, I began hearing
about Melvin. Melvin had been convicted of fishing violations

including an over-limit of walleyes resulting in his loss of fishing privileges for a year. The local conservation officer knew him and briefed me on his past. A number of the new sportsmen I met asked when I was going to catch Melvin. It seemed lots of people believed Melvin was still over-limit fishing.

One summer I received specific information about Melvin's fishing activities from an anonymous source. The facts were specific enough that I formulated a plan to gather details about Melvin's actions to charge him or clear him. I enlisted the help of neighboring officers and spent additional days on the lake, both in and out of uniform. I even found a willing neighbor who allowed me to observe Melvin's dock when he came to shore. I was finally able to document what types and numbers of fish he brought back. Surveillance was done on nearly a daily basis. I knew Melvin went to his out-of-state home in the middle of every week, and I suspected he stored fish at his elderly mother's out-of-state residence as well as his own.

I realized Melvin was a creature of habit. He fished at least once a day when conditions allowed; he fished the same locations and usually fished alone. When other boats came near Melvin, he would move on to another favorite spot.

I continued to make observations all summer until I decided I had enough information by Labor Day weekend to make a move. After I saw Melvin take the boat out of the water, I believed his fishing was over for the season. I arranged for a neighboring officer and an out-of-state game warden to assist with searches if it came to that.

I knew Melvin was at his lake home alone, so I decided to pay a visit. When Melvin answered my knock, I asked if I could come in and talk. After taking a seat in Melvin's living room, I told him that his fishing activity was the subject of an ongoing investigation. I asked Melvin if he had fish stored in the lake home, and he admitted to having 16, four walleyes over the possession limit. I asked if he had fish stored anywhere else and he became quiet. I asked if he had fish stored at his mother's house. Melvin appeared surprised at the question and admitted there were more fish there. I asked if there were fish stored at his North Dakota home and he said there were. When I asked how many fish he had, he lowered his eyes and quietly admitted he had a lot of fish. I told Melvin there were officers contacting his mother about fish stored at her home, and he expressed concern for his frail elderly mother's health. I suggested he call her. Melvin did call his mother and asked her to cooperate with the officers.

Melvin continued to be cooperative, and I asked him if he would go to his home in North Dakota and turn over the fish he had in possession. He agreed if he could ride in the patrol vehicle and get a ride back. Of course I was agreeable.

While driving to Melvin's home, he was talkative. He explained that every week he and his wife would leave the lake with 12 walleyes and store them at the permanent home. He said he took many of the fish to Arizona where he would put on fish fries for friends. Melvin discussed his 29 years of experience on the lake and his knowledge of where and how to fish for walleyes. He stated he only fished the one lake and in summer only.

We arrived at Melvin's permanent home where a Minnesota conservation officer and a North Dakota game warden met us. Melvin showed us a freezer filled with packages of frozen fish. A total of 35 packages containing six walleyes each were seized as well as five packages obtained from Melvin's mother. In all, Melvin was found to possess 560 walleye fillets over his limit.

On the drive back to his lake home, Melvin was very concerned with what was going to happen. He said the revocation of fishing privileges was an awful experience. I tried to put his anxieties to rest as best I could. I told him that when I went to work that morning I knew I was going to conclude the investigation and that if there were more than 100 walleyes over limit, I was going to see that his new boat and motor were confiscated. I reconsidered that position and told Melvin that because he was cooperative, I was not going to take the boat and would not revoke his fishing privileges. I also agreed to decide as soon as possible what he would be charged with.

The next day another officer and I returned to Melvin's lake home and met with him and his wife. We discussed the case and decided to issue one summons with a payable amount of $3,690. When Melvin heard the amount, he turned to his wife and said, "Write the check." The deal was done.

Since the days of Melvin's case, Minnesota has toughened the penalties for such cases. Today the same case would require the forfeiture of the boat, motor and trailer. The loss of fishing privileges would be immediate and would be for all DNR licenses for five years. The criminal penalty would now be a gross misdemeanor with up to a $3,000 fine and a year in jail. Restitution to the State would be $7,125 in addition to the fine.

Melvin's over-limit fishing conviction was well publicized in the outdoor world. I had decided to visit with Melvin after the dust settled when he returned from his winter in Arizona. Just before I was planning to stop, Melvin called me. He said he wanted me to stop by the lake home, so I paid Melvin a visit a couple days later. He related how he had some awful experiences after his story was published. He received nasty calls and letters from all over. In an attempt to prove that his violations were now in the past, I suggested we go fishing together. I wanted an opportunity to show him how to catch and release a fish, something I knew was foreign to his nature. Melvin said he'd like to do that and he'd show me his secret fishing spots. I agreed to meet him on the lake the next morning.

Another officer and I located Melvin on the water. He was alone in his boat and said he went out a little earlier and already had five walleyes. He showed us another location where walleyes were probably located. I caught a walleye almost immediately and got Melvin's attention as I released it. Melvin then caught another walleye that went into the live-well. We all acknowledged he had his limit. Melvin baited up again and put his line down. It wasn't long before he had another walleye on. When he looked at us and asked what he should do, we said he needed to release it. Melvin was shocked. He said, "But I'm party fishing with you." We pointed out that party fishing is only allowed if you are fishing in the same boat. Melvin responded, "Well then, get in my boat!" And the off-duty officer with me did just that. Melvin showed us a number of good fishing locations, and the fishing went on until we had a limit of fish. Catch-and-release is probably still a difficult concept for Melvin to grasp, but I have no reason to believe he violates any fishing laws today.

A number of years have passed since the incident described, but I continue to make it a point to stop by Melvin's house a couple times a summer. He's always glad to see me.

Dennis Lang is a 25 year veteran conservation officer and is currently stationed in Perham, Minnesota as a sergeant. He is also a field training officer and background investigator. Dennis served in the Minnesota Army National Guard for 21 years as an officer and helicopter pilot and for many years was a volunteer firefighter.

TWENTY FOUR
The Deer Camp

Long-established hunting traditions in Minnesota, and most other states for that matter, have always included large tracts of privately owned land where hunting and fishing are controlled by a well-to-do landlord or corporation. These "camps" have provided decades of recreational enjoyment not only for the owners but equally for the guests, some who have hunted for so many years that their annual invitations are taken for granted. Many of these groups have semi-formal rules stating the *dos* and *don'ts* during a stay, a few even charging membership fees.

Itasca County is dotted with camps of all sizes and purposes. Some are occupied only during waterfowl season, others are strictly used for deer hunting or just fishing. A small number comprise a combination of all three activities. Only a few enclose a thousand acres or more of private timber and lakes with no access by the public.

The bulk of these private estates are owned and operated by law-abiding folks who recognize the value and appeal of the special property that has been entrusted to them. The few negative encounters I've experienced dealt mostly with members who became insensitive to the public's right to utilize the public waters adjoining their camps. Following a bit of education, I found most of the groups were willing to get in step with the rules.

After four years in the Grand Rapids station, I redirected my patrol strategy to include added attention to parcels of private land that I suspected hadn't been visited by a game warden in the recent past. My first step was to lay out a plat map of my patrol district and identify potential sites by size, ownership, and building locations. I had learned early on that the more inaccessible and isolated the residence or camp, the greater the likelihood of game and fish violations. It takes a continuous and conscious effort by everyone to behave; otherwise, over time, there is a tendency to bend the rules and minimize their importance. Most hunting camps that have a dominant leader who isn't afraid to step up and declare his intolerance for shaky conduct will very seldom be a problem.

One bright afternoon on the fifth day of deer season, I selected a site that met all my qualifications of remoteness and degree of difficulty for property access. Only 18 miles north of town, I guessed I could walk in unannounced, check the place out and return home before dark. It is a huge, 5,000-plus-acre private setting, completely wooded and dotted with numerous undisturbed lakes. I knew little about the ownership or history of this magnificent chunk of pristine terrain other than what I heard from area folks. Apparently the owners were the third generation of a pioneer logging, farming, and mining family from the Duluth area, and according to my confidants, appeared to be good stewards of the land. I certainly had no preconceived notions of any irregularities and looked forward to introducing myself and meeting the individuals in charge.

I had a habit of always wanting to make my first visit to any new camp a surprise. If everything was in order upon my appearance, that was great! I thought it also added credibility to the job; showing up completely unexpected was a great deterrent, influencing behavior many years into the future. On the other hand, if there were any violations noted, I certainly wouldn't have been able to discover them if they knew I was coming.

With packsack strung over a shoulder, I started my long hike. The entire area was crisscrossed with old logging trails and one major access road connecting the north and south entrances. Three miles from each gate was the main lodge my final objective. Surrounding the entire acreage were large no-trespassing signs marking the perimeter and announcing the fact that the uninvited public was unwelcome. Being private land, this was certainly the prerogative of the owner to keep hunters out that hadn't attained permission, and the trespass laws supported his right. In fact, trespassing was such a problem that the caretaker's full-time job during the 16-day deer season was to patrol the boundaries by jeep looking for hunters encroaching on the property. If I were the landowner, I would have probably taken the same approach.

Of course, if a person wanted to sneak through the area unseen—such as the local game warden—the major obstacle would obviously be that same caretaker . . . in his little jeep! I was just finding the rhythm of my stride when I heard approaching engine noise. Walking along the main road was the easiest and quickest way in, but I certainly wanted to remain undetected at the same time. Tramping through the woods at 3:00 p.m. was no option considering the amount of daylight left, so I would have to dodge whatever traffic I encountered—not exactly easy while wearing a blaze orange coat and hat! I wasn't going to take the chance of traversing three miles of prime hunting land, most likely packed with hunters, wearing camouflage. I wanted to accomplish my goal, but I also needed to return home without unsolicited holes!

The engine clamor increased until I had little choice but to head for the woods. Whoever it was, they were slowly coming in my direction around a curve ahead of me. I had a momentary lapse of thought while I was stumbling over logs and crashing through the leafless brush until I recalled my blaze orange clothing. "I have to get down like right now!" I dove for an aging white pine stump, figuring it would shield my blazing form enough to block an approaching view. I dared not move or even look up for fear of detection until the rumbling passed completely by. When the noise began to fade, I popped my head up over the stump in time to see the rear end of an open-top, quarter-ton jeep . . . my arch-rival and "obstacle of the day" . . . the dreaded caretaker! I pondered the situation and how contrary it was to my usual mode of operation: "Instead of the pursuer, I've become the pursuee. Now there's a twist. This guy was basically looking for me!" For a moment, I felt a mutual respect for his profession. But that thought passed quickly, and it was back to work.

I figured I had gone only about a mile when, once more, I recognized the semi-muffled exhaust coming up from behind at a quicker pace than I was able to adjust for—he was on me right now! I made a 90-degree plunge for a clump of alder brush, clutching the bottom stems and pulling myself as low to the ground as I could. "I'm only 10 feet off the road and look like a beacon," I thought. "He's got me now!" To my complete amazement, the little machine drifted by without the slightest change in speed. He had missed me again!!

"I'm not going to get a third shot at this . . . I've got to move at a faster pace. Couple more miles shouldn't be a problem," I contemplated as I hugged the right side of the roadway.

Not even ten minutes later, I heard another approaching vehicle. "Can't be him again," I thought. "If it is, he's certainly earning his pay. I'll have to pass that on to his boss if I ever meet him. It's like the man knows I'm out here." It was him alright, plodding along at his own pace. I felt I was pretty well hidden on this pass but knew he'd be coming up from behind in the next few minutes. His MO wasn't hard to figure out.

I was right. Back into the brush and under a conifer I leaped. One thing I noticed on this pass was that my inquisitive care-taker member wasn't actually looking around much. I gave him an "A" for persistence but a "D" for alertness on his performance review. "Another half mile and I'll be at my target," I thought. Wrong. Yet again he putted by while I hugged the opposite side of a 3-foot diameter white pine. (The many 100-year or older white pine trees on this property can only be described as magnificent.) Now I had to wait for his return. His status had just advanced from annoying pest to major nuisance.

As he lumbered by in the direction of the lodge for the third time, I pretty much jogged the rest of the distance to the steps of the cabin. A lodge, a cabin, a home . . . whatever one would choose to call it, the building was attractive, a postcard scene from the past. I assumed the caretaker was patrolling the south road, so I walked up and knocked on the inside door adjacent to the kitchen. A mild-mannered woman inside invited me to step in.

"Game Warden," I announced. "Just checking camps today. Do you happen to have a tag for that deer you're cutting up?" Up to her elbows in blood and tallow, the lady whimpered, "We got one. Just haven't put it on yet."

"How about right now?" I strongly suggested. "Then we're even. Any other deer around here?"

"I think there's one hanging in back," she answered in a meek voice. "Just behind the screen house."

"Are you any connection to the guy riding around in the jeep?" I asked.

"That's my husband. We're the caretakers here. He should be back any minute." Just as I hit the bottom step, around the corner came the jeep. As the driver spied me, he drove up closer and stopped, unsure of who I was. As he studied the patch on my arm and suddenly noticed the badge, his demeanor quickly turned to shock, his eyes appearing to double in size. "How . . . how in the heck did you get in here? Where did you come from . . . where's your car?"

The poor guy was on the brink of losing control. Somebody had slipped in underneath his radar, and he took it as the ultimate insult. It was my time to have a little fun. "I just walked in from the north gate," I stated bluntly. "Where were you? Thought I might run into you on the trail."

That pretty well did it. "That's impossible . . . what . . . where . . . I don't get it! I was all over that road."

"No big deal," I stated. "Just here to check any deer you might have around the place. Are there others out hunting?"

"Yeah, they'll be back about 5:00 p.m., about eight hunters," he grumbled. "There's a deer hanging behind the cabin."

There was indeed a deer hanging along the outside of the screened porch. There was also no tag attached as required by law when in camp. This is not a huge violation, but the purpose of the rule is to identify the hunter and the corresponding license under which the deer was taken. The deer then becomes the legal possession of that person and reduces the deceptive manipulation of licenses otherwise possible while party hunting. In other words, the law is a good enforcement tool to help guarantee equality and fairness in the field.

As I cut the deer down, I explained to the caretaker that I would wait for the members of the hunting party to come in from the woods and would talk to them all at that time.

"Shouldn't be long now," he mumbled. "It's almost dark." He appeared worried, as if his job was on the line . . . and I wasn't quite sure it wasn't.

As the last of the group walked up to the cabin, they greeted me with friendly smiles and handshakes. It was obvious these men were not hardcore poachers. In fact they all appeared conscientious and straightforward, like the majority of the hunting community. After checking their licenses, I informed them of the untagged deer. "Somebody is going to have to take responsibility," I stated. "Who's going to step up and claim the animal?"

Following a short huddle, one of the members moved forward and said he would take the ticket. "Thank you, Senator. I appreciate your forthrightness."

"Yeah, we got a little careless. I guarantee you, it won't happen again!"

I believed him. They appeared to be a good bunch and just needed a little nudge to get them back to legal ground. I was satisfied!

"Where are you parked?" one of them inquired.

"Out at the north gate," I responded, slightly feigning a dejected look.

"That's way too far to drag a deer. Give the officer a ride back to his car, please," the Senator directed toward the caretaker. "Throw the deer on the back of the jeep."

You can just about guess how much conversation transpired on the way out to the gate. My driver was not in any mood to even look in my direction, much less talk. He kept his somber mood as I unloaded the deer. The last I saw of him was his hasty retreat back to the camp. Rumors have it that was the end of his career as a deer camp surveillance coordinator.

Addendum: A thank you to the new owner of this estate, Jack Rajala, and his ceaseless commitment and dedication to the re-establishment of White Pine trees in Minnesota and throughout the country.

A beautiful rustic lodge located in the heart of Itasca County.
(Owner Jack Rajala)

TWENTY FIVE
The Dam-Site Sneakers

Every game warden who has ever lived has come into contact with illegal fishing activity near a dam. No matter the size, dams are natural attractors for all species of fish that live near these man-made barriers. The shallow, oxygenated basins below most dams provide perfect habitat for large numbers of spring spawning fish. The fast moving spring runoff waters from the melting ice of connected lakes and rivers serve as a "draw" that fish cannot resist. Of course, these conditions are just what the doctor ordered for the "unscrupulous" among us who would take advantage of fish during their most vulnerable time of the year. Itasca County was no exception!

A private dam that provides power and water for the local paper-mill is the first barrier for almost 100 miles upstream from Brainerd, Minnesota, on a relatively narrow section of the Mississippi River. Less than 100 feet wide, the dam holds back between 10 and 15 feet of water. Excess water flows through its spillways at various cubic meters per second depending on area rainfalls throughout the seasons. Not only do fish accumulate in huge numbers below this structure, but walleyes and other species, including muskies, will swim downstream and appear above the dam near the walls of the adjoining mill utility buildings.

It didn't take long as a member of the Grand Rapids community to gather "hints" on some of the goings-on that had been and were most likely still taking place at this dam site during the spring fish run. Besides a couple of my predecessors, most information came from acquired friends and those who had been "in the know" for some time. I even heard that guards were stationed to "watch for the warden" during the swift excursions back and forth from the dam to the plant with illegally speared fish. It was time to go to work to confirm or dispel these statement and rumors.

My friend Bill volunteered to assist with me this early spring evening. Our only goal this first night was to find a surveillance location near the dam that would not only provide a total view of the adjacent buildings but could also afford us a good chance to quickly apprehend a violator. We found the ideal site just off the south side of the structure under a group of large spruce trees that helped shield us from the dim orangish rays of the overhead security lights. We could observe the entire length of dam, the upper building structure with its two doorways opening out to the top of the dam, and also the cement catwalk running along the water's edge 10 feet below the top edge. This walkway eventually wound around two corners and ended at another door into the plant.

As we watched for the first hour, we discussed preliminary plans on what actions we would take if we would see someone spearing fish from the various access sites. I also told Bill that I would be committing a few hours every night for the next week to this venture and that his assistance was very much appreciated.

Just past 1:00 a.m., it appeared my week of planned surveillance was about to come to an end the first night. Glancing at the catwalk below, I could barely discern a shadowy figure out-lined against the gray cement wall. "Bill, I think we've got some-body below us on the opposite side. See. Over there." I pointed my binoculars in that direction and focused on an individual halfway along the 20-foot narrow walkway with a flashlight in one hand and a 6-foot spear in the other. I could see a thick rope draped over his shoulders and attached to the end of the spear. "This is going to be a tough capture," I whispered to Bill. "I'm going to have to low-crawl across the top of the dam and work my way over to the platform just above him . . . without being detected. Why don't you wait here and come quick once I make contact with him."

The walkway across the top of the dam consisted of a sharp, tooth-like corrugated steel tread-way. The first 20 feet of my stealthy creep removed all the buttons on my shirt and my badge and was starting to wear through my undershirt. I couldn't see my prey along the route, but if I had lifted my head, there would have been a good chance he would have seen my movements since he was almost directly facing the dam in his search for fish. After reaching the end of the jagged path with my shirt shredded like a hurricane-battered flag, I slithered down a short flight of steps leading to a railing 8 feet above the perpetrator.

"This should be less complicated from here on," I thought. "I'll just cast a light on him from above and order the gentleman to remain in place."

"Easier said than done!" That wasn't the first time I'd mut-tered this phrase just before a fine-tuned plan turned sour. "Game warden!" I shouted above the noise of the roiling water as I lit up his head and shoulders with my six-cell flashlight. "Stay put! Don't move!! I'll be right down."

Most of the time, people caught in situations like this are either too petrified to move, or they just give up and wait for the inevitable. I said "most"! He, however, was one of the rare exceptions. I felt I could read his mind during the those next six seconds. I'm sure he was thinking, "I could give up and prepare for the complete humiliation, ridicule and dishonor that would be heaped on me by my fellow workers, and most likely follow me through the rest of my career as having the distinction of being the only person in recent memory to be caught at the plant taking illegal fish. Or, I could make a run for it."

He decided the latter!! With one big heave, he sent the spear flying into the deep pool below the dam apron and almost immediately flung his flashlight into the darkness. He then turned and raced along the cement ledge toward the first corner.

"Don't do it," I shouted. "I know who you are!" Of course, I had no idea who he was, but I thought I'd try the last tool in my box to stop the man. Didn't work! Around the first corner and around the second he ran. He was now within 30 feet of a door as I hurtled myself over the railing, dropping six feet to the ramp below. I knew if I landed in front of him, it was going to be an all-out one-on-one. It didn't happen! I landed just after he shot between my dropping legs. By the time I turned around, the door had banged shut. I dashed to the handle, flung the door open and was greeted by a group of straight-faced employees who had suddenly acquired a case of lockjaw. Searching a building of that size was fruitless. I'd been beat, and I knew it.

"I think we're out of luck," I hollered up to Bill. "Unless you recognized the guy, we're done for the night."

"Nope. Everything happened so fast, I didn't even get a chance to get here in time."

"Maybe I'll go have a talk with some folks tomorrow," I added to Bill. "I'll have a talk with the management, too."

I didn't get a chance. My first phone call the following morning was from plant security. I was scolded and warned for not wearing a hard hat when I had entered the plant for those few seconds. "Unbelievable," I thought. Nobody gives a rip for the rules of fishing, only for the fact that I had broken an in-house safety rule by not donning head protection prior to chasing one of their own employees into the plant who had just committed a crime. I hung up in amazement but later made a visit to management. I was listened to politely enough, but a subtle aura of indifference permeated the conversation. I doubt if the next day's posted notice, announcing that dam fishing walleyes out of season would not be tolerated, was really taken that seriously. It's hard to put an end to long-standing traditions.

Another encounter with violators near the dam occurred the night before a fishing season opener. Traditionally, fishermen in waders line the banks below the dam a couple of hours before midnight to secure their walleye fishing spot. Many could be seen casting, sometimes catching and releasing fish in the darkness. Although illegal to possess the fish before 12:00 a.m., it is not a violation to catch and then release walleyes.

As I crept down the steep, rocky bank, I could see the silhouetted outlines of five people, each with rod in hand, reeling and casting into the 6-foot pool of water. Occasionally a fish would be caught, but the almost total darkness obscured whether the fish were being released or kept. I had a feeling that this group was not returning the fish because of what I thought to be rope stringers hanging in the water from each fisherman's belt. My binoculars would only do so much in the blackness, but I thought it worthwhile to approach the group from the rear . . . and check them for early fish.

As I tiptoed closer and closer on the jutting rocks, I was amazed how near I was getting to the whole crew. I would have to enter the cold water, without the benefit of waterproof footwear, and close the gap before they detected my presence and released their stringers into the darkness. Only 2 feet behind the middle fisherman, I could see walleye tails roiling on the surface next to them in the waist-high river. They were, in fact, starting the season early. It wasn't fair to those who were waiting patiently for midnight, so I made the decision right there to capture as many as I could. I would just grab all their stringers at one time . . . and reel them in toward shore.

Unfortunately, once again a tactic of mine turned into quite a fiasco. I reached out and grasped the middle stringer with my right hand, reached to my left and grabbed a second rope, transferred the first stringer to my left hand and struggled for another to my right and finally clutched a third rope. I now had the middle three fishermen pretty much at my mercy before they realized what was happening. "Game Warden!" I shouted. "Just slowly back out of the water; I've got you by the pants. I want to check your licenses."

Next, the splashing of water from the other fishermen in the area as they attempted to clamber to shore with their rods flying and feet slipping on the rocks could be heard even above the noise from the dam. The other two of my poaching quintet took off in opposite directions, but I held tightly to my three prizes.

They were so off balance because of the pressure I was applying to their belts that they had trouble getting out of the water, let alone trying to escape. As I landed my three violators on the shoreline rocks, I realized that I also was dragging in a large catch of walleyes at the same time.

"OK, OK, you got us," one of them mumbled. "We'll just sit down here." The pressure of stumbling in reverse and the weight that was attached to each of them had pooped them out as much as I was. We all sat on the rocks while my flashlight lit up the full stringers of fish lying next to us. "You guys have done pretty well, but you're a little early," I declared. "Why don't you all dig out your licenses."

They were all cooperative and very curious how I could have gotten so close to them.

"You were too absorbed in your fishing . . . and you're not the only one who uses the cover of darkness," I said. (He's here! He's there! He's everywhere! So beware!)

They had a total of 35 walleyes. Not only were they all preseason fish, but each person was also over his daily limit. Following the paperwork, I dragged the 35 walleyes over the bridge and 4 blocks to a holding tank for the "Pike-for-Vets" program. I hope our disabled veterans enjoyed them.

A federal dam on the Mississippi River, just two miles upstream from the downtown dam in Grand Rapids, was another site of continuous enforcement activity. Many people stop to picnic or camp along this stretch of river. At least a half dozen times a year, I would be involved in some type of foot chase with folks without fishing licenses. Most were fishing on the opposite side of the river from the parking area so they could watch for any approaching uniformed personnel. Many were nonresidents who would take a chance without a license as they passed through the area and used this site as a rest stop. My normal tactic was simply to stop my walk halfway across the dam, and stand for a time in full uniform. It usually didn't take long to establish who was illegal. Those without the proper licenses would slowly slip away from their equipment and later deny ownership, or they would drop their rods and reels and dash into the woods behind them.

I became so accustomed to this type of behavior that I would sometimes glance at the value of the rods left behind during the ensuing pursuit and decide whether it was worth continuing the chase. In many instances, the value of the rod and reel combos would exceed the fine for the violation. I would then terminate the chase and gather up the equipment, eventually adding more items to the state auction.

This dam was also a target for fishing shenanigans after dark. Huge walleyes, northern pike and muskies would arrive in the spring for spawning and lie just below the dam's discharge areas in easy reach of a spear or snag hook. I was always on the lookout for movement on or near the opposite side of the dam in the late spring evenings and early morning hours.

One night on my way home at 2:00 a.m., I made my normal stop just beyond the parking lot and walked back to look at the dam with binoculars. I immediately saw an individual standing on the cement barrier attempting to snag fish. I sneaked across the driveway and positioned myself behind a small round pump house about 20 feet from the dam walkway and waited. Soon, I could hear his noisy footsteps on the metal ramp as he approached my hiding spot. The instant the clomping noise stopped, I counted to six, which was the time it would take to cover the remaining distance, and quickly stepped from behind the shelter. His next step was directly into my face. "Game Warden. What are you up to this fine spring evening?" I'm not sure what my poacher was thinking at that moment, but observing his startled demeanor, I was again convinced there's something to be said for using surprise tactics. After his shaking stopped and his bodily functions returned to normal, he caught his wind and softly mumbled, "Nothing. Just stopped to look at the fish."

I've been watching you do a little more than just admire the fish," I affirmed as my flashlight revealed a familiar face. "What the heck are you doing out here this time of night? My gosh, how do you get enough sleep when you're out walking all day?!"

I was staring at my favorite mailman!

TWENTY SIX
The Hijacking

It was 5:54 a.m. when I checked in with the State Patrol dispatcher to begin my day working duck hunting activity. I was immediately informed of a "situation" involving one of my fellow officers which included a civilian attempting to call in on the warden's radio. I quickly contacted my supervisor, Don Fultz, and we started our 50 mile race to the scene.

The following radio transmission was taken word-for-word from the 18 page State Patrol radio log and were the first words heard by the dispatcher: "This is an Emergency. Emergency. Emergency. Can you get some help up here, help us here. We had an accident with the game warden. We're still at the car. I don't know. We heard a couple of shots. We're still at the car." Don and I were the first officers to arrive.

The following account was written by friend and retired Minnesota Conservation Officer Lonnie Schiefert after examining the transcript of the incident for the first time in 20 years. "It brings back some unpleasant memories, and I didn't expect the effect it would have on me," he writes. Officer Schiefert was stationed in Northome, Minnesota from 1971 to 1980. This is his story.

October 3, 1975, started normal in every way for a young enthused conservation officer in the northwoods of Minnesota. Duck season had just started, and the days were getting shorter and cooler. I had been stationed in Northome for about four years and knew the area and the people quite well. From talking to residents and other officers in the area I became well aware that deer poaching or "shining" was a popular activity for some local citizens at this time of year. Dealing with it was a constant challenge for all the old-time game wardens, and I always enjoyed listening to them tell stories about cases they had made or about the ones that got away. I didn't know it then, but in a few years I would have many stories of my own to tell.

About October, I was told by a citizen that there had been shooting and shining of deer off County Road 29 about 5 miles east of Alvwood. This wasn't surprising news but just another bit of information that goes into the decision-making process an officer uses to decide where to work. County Road 29 is known as the Dora Lake Road, and the area is mostly woods with a few farm fields. I didn't mind the long hours of night work and had heard it described as hours of boredom interrupted by moments of excitement. I had developed a method of staying out all night. I used a sleeping bag on a foam rubber pad on the hood of my patrol car; this gave me reasonable comfort and some rest. The heat from the engine also added warmth. This way I could hear things that couldn't be heard from inside a car, and I am sure I fell asleep many times only to wake up when a car went by or a shot was fired.

On October 1, I was involved in a shining case that required a trip to the lab in St. Paul, Minnesota. When I got back, I talked to my neighboring officer about staking out the Dora Lake Road. He was tired and he knew I was tired from my long day, so he suggested I go home and get some rest. It was good advice and I took half of it. I knew it would be better to have two officers for this activity, but I believed that my badge made me bulletproof. I decided to stake out the alfalfa field the citizen complaint had indicated, and I crawled into my warm, comfortable sleeping bag. My stakeout started in the evening about eight or nine. My plan was to spend the night there and just see what went on. I always had the Highway Patrol radio on and probably slept off and on, especially after midnight when there were few radio transmissions or little car traffic on the road. It was a calm, cold night, and I could hear the sounds of the night from far off. About 5:00 a.m. a car came from the west, and I could hear it slow down as it passed by the alfalfa field that usually had from one to a dozen deer. I was fully awake when I heard a shot fired less than a quarter mile away. I threw my sleeping bag on the ground, got into my car and headed out to the road with lights out.

When I got to the road, I could see a car to the west sitting crossways in the roadway shining its lights on the field to the north. I drove west without lights until I was almost to them and then turned on my headlights and flashing red light. They turned toward me and as we neared each other I could see that they were not going to stop, so I set up a roadblock by parking crosswise on the road. They tried to get around me by taking the shoulder, so I cut them off and they rammed into the passenger side of my patrol vehicle. After I got out of the car with my flashlight, I could see that there were four of them and the driver and front seat passenger were getting out and coming toward me. As they approached, I asked for identification, and as they were getting it out and handing it to me, I saw the passenger in the right seat crawl out the window and walk away. He was walking stiff-legged, so I thought maybe he had been injured. The other back seat passenger was walking with him, east into the darkness. I left the two I had identified and followed the others down the road. I told them to stop, but they continued walking until we were about a hundred yards from the cars.

At this time I discovered why he was walking stiff-legged; he was concealing a shotgun behind his leg so I couldn't see it. He turned around and pointed the gun at me and told me to get on the ground and spread my arms and legs out or he would blow my head off. He reached under my coat and removed my pistol and took my flashlight. Both of them went back to talk to the others and I could hear parts of the conversation. They were trying to get a car going, and I heard one say something about, "buying us some time." The one with the gun came back to me and told me to look at the birch trees in the woods and to walk in that direction and that he wanted to hear brush cracking for a half hour. I then started thinking I might make it out alive. Before that I was thinking about my 4-year-old son. I crossed the ditch into the woods and walked what I thought was a safe distance into the brush. I could hear pounding noises back at the cars. While I sat down and tried to calm myself, I looked up at the stars to see what direction I needed to go to get to the nearest farm.

When I started moving again, I knew I had to go about a half mile to the west, so I started walking through the woods in the dark without a flashlight. I remembered the order I had been given to make noise for a half hour, but I also knew I was far enough away to be safe. I recognized the noise back on the road as they tried to get one of the cars going. The fenders were jammed into the tires; both cars were incapable of being moved. If either car had been drivable, I believed they would have left the scene. They thought they could get a car going when they sent me into the woods. My problem now was to navigate through the trees and cross a small creek. Some odd thoughts from my upbringing came to mind. My dad would have said, "Don't get your shoes wet." I was able to get down the bank, cross the water and climb up the other side. The rest of the way was just stumbling through the woods until I reached a farm yard. I knew the farmer and he knew me. I wondered what he was thinking when I woke him up and asked if I could borrow his gun. I knew he didn't have a phone, but he gave me a gun, and I headed out the driveway to the next farm.

At this time I heard a lot of shooting, and in my confusion I thought that the poachers were shooting at passing cars. I got to the next farm house, and instead of knocking on the door, for some reason I went around to the kitchen window and tapped on it where I saw the lady was up and working over the kitchen sink. She recognized me and motioned me to come on in. I called the Highway Patrol dispatcher and told him not to send anyone here unless they had help. Sometime later I realized that the shooting I had heard was just early morning duck hunters.

Officers started arriving soon, and a car was sent to pick me up. The two poachers I had identified were still there, but the other two poachers were gone. While I had been gone, one of the poachers had taken it upon himself to call the dispatcher on my patrol car radio and relate the situation. (The poacher told the dispatcher that the collision was accidental and that the warden took off running down the road.) With dozens of officers from the Itasca County Sheriff's office, State Patrol and conservation officers from as far as 50 miles away, and a plane and a helicopter, there was a ground search for the two remaining culprits which I took part in until early afternoon. I was then taken to Grand Rapids to give a statement to sheriff deputies and to pick up a different patrol car. By late afternoon we received word via radio that the missing poachers had been found and were being driven to the county jail. I was to meet them there to identify them. I then headed home and learned that my wife had been notified I was OK. The "OK." was only partly right; my head was messed up and continued that way for many months. If this incident had happened in later years, there would have been some debriefing and some psychological help, but as it was back then, I was on my own.

Months later when it came time for trial, we started to pick a jury, and it was decided they would plead guilty to kidnapping, aggravated assault and deer shining. One was given 16 months in prison, but the others got less. When it came time to dispose of confiscated equipment, one defendant told me I shouldn't have worried as much because the shotgun with which I had been threatened often misfired. I later received a letter from the man in prison. I think it was a forced apology as a condition of his release from Stillwater State Prison.

On reflection, I never figured out for sure why two of them called for help on the radio. It might have been due to the fact

8 B
Minneapolis Tribune
Tues., Oct. 7, 1975

4 charged in warden kidnapping

Associated Press

Grand Rapids, Minn.
Four Minnesota men were arraigned in Grand Rapids Monday on charges of kidnapping and three other counts in connection with the alleged disarming and kidnapping of a game warden.

The four who appeared before Itasca County Judge William Spooner are Ronald G. McGrath, 36, 800 E. Cook Av., St. Paul; Alexander Schaaf, 40, Ball Club; his brother Francis D. Schaaf, 30, 300 E. 15th St., Minneapolis, and Alexander Schaaf's son Ralph, 18, Ball Club.

Itasca County authorities charged them with kidnapping, aggravated assault with a dangerous weapon, illegally hunting deer and theft of the warden's pistol.

All were released on $10,000 bond each, said Assistant County Attorney Larke Huntley. He said they were scheduled to appear in court next Monday.

Warden Lonnie Schiefert, not home, said he was driving along a county road in northern Itasca County Friday morning and noticed someone hunting deer from a car.

He said he tried to stop the vehicle but that the two cars collided and that he was forced to lie down on the road on orders of one of the men who came out of the other vehicle armed with a gun.

"They said they'd blow my head off if I didn't," Schiefert said.

He said he was forced by two of the men to walk ahead of them into the woods, and that he fled and was able to reach a farmhouse and notify officers.

A Minneapolis Tribune press article detailing the warden kidnapping.

I had their identification in my possession, but I had no way of knowing who the others were. On the question of how serious they were about using the shotgun, I can only say I took it totally seriously! I could only hear parts of the conversation they were having as I was lying on the road more than 50 yards away. I don't remember any conversation between them and me. As I think about it now, the order was unconditional, "Do as you are told or else!" I also believe drunkeness was a factor as I learned they had been drinking until the wee hours of the morning and then decided to go "hunting."

Tom, this is what happened to the best of my recollection.

Lonnie Schiefert joined the Minnesota Division of Enforcement as a Conservation Officer in May 1970 and was assigned to Austin as his first station. Mr. Schiefert was also stationed at Northome, Henning and Fergus Falls where, since his departure in 1998, he operates his own hobby farm. He enjoys traveling and has built two houses in retirement.

TWENTY SEVEN
The Dam Walleyes

In the spring of 2001, I decided to conduct the last prefishing season operation of my career in a remote spot where I had always suspected illegal fishing for walleyes before season. I had held this operation in reserve for a couple of reasons: I took for granted it would be a successful gamble due to the lack of enforcement presence for decades in that location, plus I thought I might collect more information during those five years. The latter never happened, but by the beginning of May, I was nonetheless making plans for a final offensive.

I needed help, though. My fellow officer colleague and professional forester buddy, Dan, jumped at the chance to volunteer as assistant and guide for our planned venture into the hinterlands the night before fishing season. Not that keeping fish a few hours before season was the most dastardly of deeds I've ever witnessed, but the act of catching and keeping a walleye with full knowledge that the season has yet to officially start is plain and simple, the raw intent to violate an easily adhered to rule.

The suspect area was a stretch of Mississippi River bank a mile south of the Winnie Dam. This structure on the outlet of Lake Winnibigoshish creates the final barrier for fish traveling north from the Mississippi River/Pokegama Lake basin. Fishing can be fabulous downstream from this government facility, so it was much more than a gut feeling that drew me to this site. The combination of isolation, inaccessibility, and fish production was a recipe for noncompliance. Besides, I knew it hadn't been visited by enforcement personnel for a long, long time.

Dan and I got there early, well before dark. In order to ensure success, we had to be able to "instantly appear" among the people who might be fishing from the banks without being seen beforehand, by anyone! The challenge was to crawl past the campsites that I was sure were set up on the trail and hills overlooking the river. All this preliminary work was absolutely necessary if we were to capture anyone in the act of catching, and most important, keeping, preseason fish.

Exiting our hidden truck, we started down the rutted trail that twisted toward our destination. The temperature had dropped to just below 40 degrees but the winds were calm, and it wasn't long before voices could be heard up ahead. Sneaking a look around the next corner, we could see vehicles and people moving about a makeshift campsite in the middle of the path. Only halfway to our objective, we already had to skirt this obstacle—forcing us into a flooded beaver impoundment of tangled cedar and spruce trees reminiscent of a movie scene in the Louisiana bayous. Topographical map in hand, Dan led the way over a bank and down into the watery quagmire.

"You sure this is the only route option we have, Dan?" I muttered after the cold water oozed over the top of my left boot, saturating my sock.

"It's the only way we can get around them," he calmly responded.

"Lead on, my trusty pathfinder," I growled as we hop-scotched from slippery logs to floating hummocks.

Now 40 minutes into our slog, it was getting darker and wetter. When the other boot filled with icy bog water, I shouted ahead to Dan, "You *do* know where you're going?"

"Yup, we're right on course. Just a short piece to go through that next marsh and we'll be up on the trail again."

Stumbling through the darkness on frozen feet in anticipation of the next sinkhole, I could hope for a successful conclusion that would make all the misery worthwhile.

"The trail is right on top of that hill," Dan whispered.

As we dragged our sapped forms over the bank, we spotted an all-terrain vehicle approaching.

"Down," I hissed to Dan. "We can't let anyone see us."

After the vehicle crawled past within feet of our prone figures, we slowly inched our way along the brushy edge and finally came within sight of the first tent. It appeared to be set up at least 50 yards from the river, so we would once again have to navigate around a site through the dense growth without being spotted by the many people standing around the campfire. The branches were so thick and the night so still that it took no time for one of the gals to hear our movements.

"What was that?" she shouted at her friend. "Over there. Maybe it's a bear. There's something in the woods. Get the flashlight."

Dan and I ever so slowly and silently assumed our prone position again. The young lady's friend flashed his light directly at us, searching for whatever may have alarmed her.

"I don't see anything," we heard him say. "It's all in your head."

I don't think she totally bought the theory, but it was enough for us to quietly continue our trek around the cluster of campers and toward our ultimate target—the banks of the river about 100 yards through the woods. This, I assumed, was where the fishing would be occurring.

"There they are, Dan," I quietly voiced. "There's at least four of them and they're all fishing. Let's just watch and listen for a while; kinda get the lay of the land."

The only illumination was the rays emitted from the two lanterns set up on top of the 8-foot river bank. Through my binoculars, the actions of the fishermen about 100 feet away were plainly visible. It didn't take long to see that walleyes were being caught and being placed on stringers with other fish already attached. Our job was to identify which of the parties were involved and then approach them with our evidence.

This all sounds like a simple enough scenario. Problem is, I've been there before. Very seldom do simple plans ever ensure easy outcomes in this business. It was one of those nights you could hear a car horn 10 miles away, and we had 50 feet of dry, 4-foot canary grass and dead leaves to crawl through prior to showing our presence. If they heard our approach, I had no doubt we'd be left with fishing rods but no one attached to them. Chasing someone into the blackness is futile, unless you want a stick in the eye and nothing else to show for it. And from my past experiences, I knew they would run.

"Let's give it a shot," I muttered to Dan lying next to me. "We'll start crawling very slowly. You approach the two on the left and just watch their actions and try to identify them. Even follow them if you have to, declaring that you're assisting the game warden. I'll grab the two on the right."

But we greatly underestimated the incredible noise emanating from the parched canary grass with even our slightest movements. The instant we started to move, one of the violators turned his flashlight on us, searching the broad field of grass where we again lay low to conceal our presence.

"Just lie still, Dan. If we don't move, he won't pick us up."

As we lay still, he got his buddy to help look for the rustling in the grass. The first guy was positive he had heard major movement but after a couple minutes pretty much gave up. We crawled again. And again, the two shone their lights in our direction. We were now so close, we could hear them breathe. It was that last 30 feet of open space that was becoming the challenge of the night.

"Whatdaya say, Dan. Let's go for it. I guarantee you they're going to take off."

As we slowly stood up, our pace picked up to a half run, kind of like those images of partially erect prehistoric ape-men. We made half the distance before all four turned and set eyes on our advancing silhouettes. Just as I assumed, there was an instant dispersal of bodies. As I rushed toward my two, I could see Dan snaring his two culprits.

"Game warden. Hold up there. Stop . . . STOP!" The nearest one ran down the bank to his rod and reel setup while the other threw his equipment and accelerated along the top of the bank directly into the blackness of the thick willow brush. I listened until the crackling and snapping died away. "At least the rest of his evening will be spent alone and cold," I reflected. "He'll be fine until he gets hungry."

My other gentleman decided he was in no position to flee. With a hangdog expression, he determined the gig was up. We both strolled over to Dan's location where a man and woman were standing stooped-shouldered next to a stringer of walleyes.

"Looks like you're 100 percent, Dan. I'm only 50. Just like I guessed, one of mine took off into the brush. He's not worth pursuing in that tangled mess." Why don't you stay here with these three and I'll work my way down the bank toward the camp. I'm sure there's more fishing going on there. I'll be right back."

In an undercover mode, I casually strolled around the corner to the rest of the group. In the darkness the four who were fishing thought I was one of them, except for a man just over the bank from where I was standing. The glow of the lantern light reflected my shadowy outline as he was unhooking a fish he had just pulled from the dark waters in front of us. With fish in hand, he headed for the stringer of walleyes anchored below me, stopping abruptly about halfway. I could almost read his mind. Was I or wasn't I one of his own? He looked up at my indifferent manner, glanced at the fish in his left hand, looked back at me, paused, looked again at his catch and knelt down slowly releasing the walleye back into the water. He just wasn't going to take a chance. Only four feet from the stringer, this guy just couldn't conquer his anxiety over my presence. "How's fishin?" I asked as I dropped down the embankment and checked the stringer at his feet.

"I don't know. Just throwin 'em back. Those aren't my fish."

That nonadmission set the stage for my next course of action. He instantly picked up on my line of work and that brought attention from the others. I basically had nothing. Of course, those were his and everybody else's fish, but due to my failure to witness anyone actively possessing them, I could never prove who caught them and put them on the stringer. I leaned over and released each fish and guided them back to the murky depths.

All I really had was a great opportunity to create a deterrent for future conduct in this locale. And isn't that really our job? They knew I knew, and that was ample satisfaction.

Strolling back to Dan, his three detainees would be charged with taking fish before season. We had observed their actions, and that could be used in court if necessary. As we arrived at the main camp, all of the tenants gathered around, mostly out of curiosity. As I issued the three summons, Dan and I learned a great deal, especially from one of the female campers. She was a 40-year-old teacher from the Twin Cities who shared with us the history of the whole camp.

According to her, this bunch of about 50 people had been meeting here on opening weekend for over 40 years! She said in a way she was glad, actually relieved, we had caught them cheating because they had been doing this for over three generations, and the guilt thing had just become too much. It just wasn't fun anymore. "Many here are related and go back to when my dad used to bring me here. I don't remember NOT fishing early. By the way," she said, "that crew that you probably passed coming in here is part of us, too. That's the other half."

I started to have good feelings about this whole expedition. My numb feet didn't matter anymore. I had accomplished something inspiring on the final opening fishing season night of my career. It was a perfect example of why enforcement and visibility is such a necessary part of managing our resources and also of why some sportsmen become indifferent to the rules if they've had little contact with enforcement personnel. These weren't bad people; they just got into a rut. I doubt if there will be any infractions in this camp for a long time.

On our way out, Dan and I walked through the other group of fishermen. It was amusing to witness the looks and hear the comments as the two of us walked by with stringers of confiscated pre-season walleyes. Of course, they hadn't yet realized what had just occurred at the neighboring camp, but they would eventually. And that was alright with us!

TWENTY EIGHT
The Curtailed Pike

Lake Winnibigoshish, or Winnie, a 58,000-acre premier walleye lake located in the heart of the Chippewa National Forest, generates enough fishing action year-round to keep four officers continuously active. Many fishermen look upon Winnie as their annual vacation destination and bring with them high expectations of success. Most activity is centered around catching walleyes which in turn supports the 12 resorts that dot the vast shoreline and adjacent Cutfoot Lakes to the east. The size-limit restrictions imposed in the last ten years have increased the average fishing hours expended to take and possess a legal daily limit.

There is no doubt the walleye is king; however, the northern pike is also a much sought-after species, especially during the peak seasons of early fall and first ice. The lake has continually produced large numbers of hefty pike despite no letup in fishing pressure. Sometimes greedy individuals become obsessive and show little regard for the rules that protect these magnificent toothy predators and assure continued quality fishing.

Late summer and early fall always signaled an adjustment in my work routine on the big lake. Knowing that this was crank-up time for northern pike production along the west and northwest shore, I slipped in that direction on a warm, tranquil afternoon. The slight westerly breeze barely rippled the surface as I approached a mixture of images reflected on the surface. Scores of boats, some motionless, others slowly dragging shimmering monofilament in their wakes, hugged the shallow waters up and down the broad shoreline. I pointed out to Hal, my civilian rider, that this would be a perfect spot to break out the lunchbox and survey the fishing action at the same time. What a perfect day it was. Soaking up the rays and watching others enjoy themselves with a backdrop of pines and glimmering water made me wonder if other working people were enjoying themselves as much as we were. I just accepted it as one of those days when it all seemed worth it. It didn't get any better than this.

But now it was time to go to work. The fishing appeared to be above average with a northern pike being boated every minute in all directions. As my binoculars scanned the various rods working the sides of the crafts, my eyes converged on one particular boat trolling by a hundred yards from us. "Let's keep an eye on that one," I mentioned to Hal. "Those three guys aren't throwing anything back, and who knows how long they've been out here." I think it was their body movements as they were fishing. Something was awry. Defining that intuition was difficult, but the combination of signs impelled me to concentrate on this particular boat over all the others. They were looking around too much, not appearing to be in an enjoyment mode and concentrating more on the fish than on the fishing. They were so serious—and fished so fast. Sounds dumb but that's another sign. Casts per minute (cpm's), I call it; it was over the top.

Another 15 minutes brought three more large pike into their boat. Of course, the limit is three per person, but only one of these can be over 30 inches. This rule was put in place to maintain the numbers of older and larger trophy sport fish that many people love to catch and many times release. I became even more suspicious when no measurement was ever taken. They also appeared to be in cahoots with another large boat. More than once the two would meet and the passengers exchange conversation—but never fish.

Their final trolling pass by us preceded their full-throttle exit toward the mouth of the Mississippi River where it pours into Lake Winnie. With less than a mile to the first of three resorts along the south banks, it was time to go. "We're going to follow them to wherever they're headed," I hollered at Hal as I started the 175 and pushed the throttle handle to the max. As we shadowed the boat, I noticed the second boat also heading in our direction. Sandwiched between the two, I made little progress in closing the gap. It didn't matter, though, as we watched the craft eventually slow and pull into a resort boat dock. Pulling up parallel to them on the opposite side of the pier, I stepped up and introduced myself. "Conservation Officer. How's the success today?" None of the occupants were very obliging, and one climbed on the dock and began walking toward the boathouse. "Hold on a second, sir. Wanna check your catch. Hang tight for a minute." As he turned and walked back, I watched the second boat pull close to the dock, turn, and then speed back out on the lake. "There's one we'll never see again," I muttered to Hal. This instantly aroused my curiosity as to what our boys had in the live-well. "Let's take a look, fellas. What ya got in there?" As I flipped open the long lid, all I saw was dark, slithering backs of large pike. The entire container was stuffed to the top with fish, big ones. "Hang close, gentlemen. I want to get a count here. Might as well take out your licenses, too." There were so many fish and so much weight that I thought it better to take them out and lay them on the grass near the dock. As Hal watched the three, I carried each pike and laid it on the ground. I wanted a picture anyway, and what better place to attract attention and send a message? The final count was 14 northern pike, nine of them were over the thirty-inch limit. "What in the world were you guys going to do with all these fish?" I asked in an unassuming tone.

"We're pre-fishing. That's all we're doing. We were going to throw them back."

"Pre-fishing what?" I questioned.

"The resort down the line is having a northern fishing contest tomorrow, and we were just checking things out."

It was blatantly obvious these fish were going to be used to cheat in the contest the next day. All three characters became silent and awkwardly submitted to the issuance of summonses for over-limits of northern pike. Sadly, the law allowed them to continue fishing the next day. Not until March of 2003 was this legislatively rectified.

The visit wasn't over. I next took a look in the community freezer. In cabin 12's bin were semi-frozen packages of huge fillets. After checking the cabin, I walked with one of the occupants back to the freezer and counted. Another over-limit. Too many fish for the number of people in the party.

As I returned to my boat after writing yet more summonses, I noticed a group of fishermen were milling around a couple stringers of walleyes on the dock. I had covered my uniform and began talking to some of the folks with the fish. They were all excited to have a picture of their catch, and not being shy, I offered to take their picture as a group. One of the guys was very reluctant and finally said no thanks and left the scene. I'm sure he had figured me out and wanted nothing to do with a game warden's photo collection. As the remaining five gathered together and hoisted the fish, I took some pretty neat pictures. I even used my personal camera. Following all the merriment, I figured it was time to drop the bomb. I removed my cover jacket and declared my status as a game warden. "Awful nice bunch of fish you have here, folks. Problem is it appears that many of them are within the "no keep" slot limit. (Slot limit in this case meant the fish that measured between 17 and 26 inches couldn't be possessed and should have been returned to the water). "Too bad I had to ruin an otherwise fun day," I thought, but they were displaying their illegal catch in front of the whole world." I was almost right on. About half the fish were too long. They all watched quietly as I measured each fish. Of course, they were very well aware of what they had. They just didn't care!

I thought it best to depart the neighborhood and take a deep breath. As we motored out into the big lake, I couldn't help thinking what I might have found in the boat that escaped earlier. Hal and I sat back and pondered what had just happened.

We agreed that we had entered an arena where compliance with the fishing laws appeared almost nonexistent. With any luck, our intrusion had spread a little education and helped create a future deterrent in that area. We only could hope!

More Lake Winnie Pike Tales

Minnesota is one of the few states that allows its residents to spear northern pike through a hole in the ice from the inside of a dark house. Thousands of winter spearing licenses are sold every year to people who spend many hours during our long winters peering down a shaft of water in the ice quietly waiting for a ghostly form to nose up to and be duped by a suspended decoy. It's one of those outdoor sports where you can enjoy a great day of fishing and stay toasty warm at the same time. Many become passionate about their unique winter activity, sometimes building sophisticated, stylish shelters and investing big bucks in specialized equipment.

Lake Winnie is considered to be one of the prime pike lakes in our state where large fish aren't unusual and taking a limit of three is almost guaranteed. December 1 is the start of the annual spearing season which runs for the next two and a half months. I always considered this day of the year to be one of my busiest. Thousands of fishermen and hundreds of shelters dotting the lake ensured a number of infractions, mostly involving over-limits and the only-one-fish-over-30-inch rule that is in effect statewide.

It was almost noon on this first day of spearing as I approached one of 60 shelters in a cluster. I had already cited several violators earlier this clear and sunny morning, so I was in a suspicious mode as I stepped gingerly up to the hinged door. "Good morning, sir," as I swung it open and gazed into the little shanty. "Just checking fish, how ya doin?" My first reaction when I saw the somewhat shaken lone occupant was one of disbelief. He was holding a rather large pike in one hand

and a pair of scissors in the other. Was he really dong what I immediately suspected? Yup! The gentleman had just cut an inch off the end of the tail. This minor surgery would reduce the fish's length below 30 inches and allow it to be included in a legal bag. The results of scissoring pike tails are also difficult to detect unless every fish is closely inspected. I never considered that a simple pair of scissors would be part of some fishermen's gear. Considering many of the things I've witnessed over the years, this one action still amazes me as to the length some people will go to intentionally defy the fishing rules.

This individual had other problems besides his customized pike. I found three other fish over 30 inches inside a bag on the floor of the house. With three large fish over the limit, I thought it was time to take a closer look at the rest of his fishing party and invest in a trip back to his rental cabin. The three other party members in two other shelters were just one fish shy of their limit. I told them I had enough reasonable suspicion to check their freezer at the resort. Just as I suspected. Seven more packages of fish, each with one fillet apiece. Just looking at the size of each fillet, it was obvious that these, too, were all over the 30-inch limit, and it was only halfway through the first day of a two-day trip for these folks.

Again, the laws prior to March 1, 2003, did not allow the seizure of their fishing licenses or revocation of privileges. They could continue to fish the next day. Also, as of this writing, game wardens, since 2002, are not allowed to enter fish shelters without permission. This case and all others cases like it could not have been made without the right to enter fish shelters when occupied. This is one of the prime court decisions that needs to be changed in order to more effectively enforce the winter fishing rules. It has created an unfair playing field for the legal sportsman.

I still believe that it's a small percentage of anglers/sportsmen who possess these cheating mindsets, but these few can do so much damage not only to the resource but also to the sense of fairness that the legal sportsman has a right to enjoy. Another justification for strong enforcement.

Over-limit of large northern pike found in a live-well day before fishing contest.

TWENTY NINE
The Moosecapades

An incoming call concerning a moose immediately leaps to the top of a warden's priority list. A moose report is usually triggered by a vehicle collision with the animal or in some cases just the mere sighting. If the animal has been freshly killed, an officer assumes immediately that a minimum of four hours of salvaging work lies ahead. The presence of a moose, dead or alive, tends to draw attention from people in general. In Itasca County, moose aren't that common, and just their sheer size and gawky appearance generate interest and curiosity. Small pockets of permanent moose populations exist in Itasca County; however, most of the sightings near the more urban neighborhoods involve animals that for some reason are itinerant visitors and are migrating from one area to another. One of the causes for this migration is the occurrence of a parasite commonly called brainworm. Although it is harmless to the whitetail deer population, it is fatal to the moose. This is one reason why larger moose populations are never common where there are high deer numbers. Animals in the final stages of this disease will act "strange," sometimes walking in circles, and are usually very approachable. When this occurs along a roadway, folks will stop to view and photograph the huge beast where it may stand for days. In many cases, an officer will dispatch the animal once it has been confirmed that the moose is a victim of the deadly sickness.

Some of the encounters I've had with moose included these and other scenarios, with each circumstance being somewhat unique. There is no moose season in Itasca County, and several incidents have included my investigation of intentional killings by the most unscrupulous of poachers.

My first experience with the demise of a moose was the opening day of deer season in the early '70s north of Nashwauk. A fellow officer, Tim, and I investigated a report of a downed bull moose lying in a field alongside a county road. We could see the black mound as we drove up, and just as we suspected, it had been shot and left to rot. After quartering the salvageable carcass, we hauled it into a grocery store where it was eventually sold to the public. This was the first of about a dozen moose that I would be called upon to investigate during the deer seasons. Rarely, a hunter would turn himself in and accept the consequences for his ineptitude in mammal identification. It's somewhat unnerving to realize that there are hunters sharing our woods who are unable to identify the difference between an 800-pound moose and a 180-pound buck deer. Formally charging an individual who willingly acknowledges his mistake is up to the officer. One case in particular that was investigated by my neighboring officer, Willy, showed that the man had shot the moose three times. In this case, there was little choice but to issue a summons, mostly for the non-statutory crime of incompetence.

A couple of townships northeast of Grand Rapids were somewhat notorious when it came to the illegal taking of big game out of season. I've mentioned before how poaching is often a generational, hand-me-down activity. No more so than in these rural areas where the occasional moose sighting prompted some of the local boys to pronounce their own moose season to be unofficially open. The "moose party-line" helped connect those who were so inclined to supplement their diet with a more exotic meat than the same old September venison they had packed away in their freezers. From the moment a moose was spotted along the wide powerline crisscrossing the entire forested region, the hunt was on until either the animal was poached or it left the area. Most of the time it was shot, quartered, and cut up within two days. I must admit that I never had the opportunity to arrest a single individual on the charge of taking a moose during closed season, but the method of operation was well known to me. I had been dealing with an informant in this area for many years who hated poaching and the constant illegal behavior that she witnessed in her neighborhood. Turning to me as her only source of assistance and eventually gaining my trust, this great lady supplied me with a vast amount of ongoing information concerning illegal game and fish activity. Many of my deer enforcement successes were directly related to this furtive relationship that also supplied facts and figures on illegal moose shootings. Knowing who was involved and where the moose meat eventually wound up was not equal to catching the culprits red-handed. They had to be caught in the acts of taking or transporting before enforcement action could be taken, and to my chagrin this opportunity never presented itself.

The closest I got to encountering some of these folks came in the form of a late night call-out to a spot smack dab in the middle of this suspect area. A cow moose had been killed by a car, and it was my job to salvage the animal. Pulling alongside the dark hump lying in the bottom of the ditch, I observed no fewer than ten people already there gazing at the carcass.

"We'd like to have it," one of them yelled as I exited the cab.

"Can't do that, boys. The rules say I have to sell it over-the-counter to the public. Sorry about that." You would have thought they had each been punched in the gut. Not a word. Just total silence in the cool night air. It was their moose in their backyard and they were entitled, is what I assumed they were thinking. My uneasiness rose a notch when I recognized one of the bystanders as a poacher who was identified by my informant. After positioning the headlights into the ditch for better vision and turning the volume up on the police radio, I exited the cab with knife in hand. After giving everything I had to roll the huge mass over, I began the tedious job of field dressing.

"Anyone care to give me a hand?" I hollered up the hill to the motionless line of human forms. I pretty much knew the answer to that question. Not a single reply. In contrast to my radio blaring into the black sky, the silence was deafening. Nobody budged and nobody left. They just stared from the shoulder as I struggled to disembowel the huge critter. Finally that job was done, and then I had to somehow get it into the back of my truck. I climbed the bank, excusing myself as I walked between two of them in order to position the truck so I could attach the winch rope to the neck. Still not a peep from anyone. Total and unrelenting silence. "Anyone want to give me a hand here, maybe run the winch motor?" I shouted.

"Don't all jump at once," I thought as I continued to fight the winch rope and the shifting weight slowly being dragged up the 6-foot slope. Amazingly the head and its trailing bulk shifted slowly into the truck box, its gangly legs protruding in every direction. A mass of sweat and bloody arms, I shifted into gear and slowly moved along the line of spectators who themselves were now beginning to leave. I have always wondered what evil intentions may have been brewing just below the surface of that hooligan-like group and exactly what specific factors may have prevented hostile behavior.

One other memorable moose event began with a call from two snowmobilers who had seen two moose jump over a bridge onto an ice-hardened river 10 feet below. Fellow Officer Dave and I headed in that direction, a very remote site 30 miles northeast of Grand Rapids, eventually unloading two snowmobiles onto the trail leading to the site of the incident. The cold frosty air and heavily laden trees at 1:00 a.m. transformed the 3-mile ride into a motorized promenade through a winter wonderland. Following behind Dave, I watched the exhaust from his machine rise and dissipate into the tall evergreens along the snowy trail. This was the essence of snowmobiling in Minnesota.

Stopping on the bridge, we spotted one of the moose lying still at the bottom of the 80-degree drop. Further inspection showed a yearling moose that had most likely died on impact in its haste to evade the approaching machines. The companion moose appeared to have survived the leap and was nowhere to be seen.

"Wadaya think, Dave? How are we going to get this up there?"

"Going to be a challenge," Dave said as he scrutinized the situation. "We'll just have to pull it up with our two machines."

"Easier said than done," I thought. Besides the steep slope, there were thick, tough branch stubs sticking up through the snow over which the carcass would have to be drug.

Our first attempts moved the critter about an inch at a time. "We need more power," I hollered. "Let's lay out the full length of both ropes and get some speed up before the ropes get taut."

About 20 of these super yanks eventually pulled the 600 pounds over the top of the sharp sticks and onto the trail. We continued the long drag back to our trucks and loaded up. Just another check-off on the list of critter rescue and salvage patrols.

As I drove back to town at 4:00 a.m., all nestled in the warmth of the cab, I reminisced about the unique situations in which officers find themselves . . . and it was good!

A moose coming under the guns of a poacher in April is very rare. Even the outlaw diehards have some appreciation for the welfare of most animals in the spring of the year, animals that have survived harsh winter conditions and are now devoted to the birth of their young.

Not necessarily so in view of one incident I handled 10 miles east of Grand Rapids. The call came in mid-morning announcing that a moose was down 50 yards south of Highway 169 and appeared to be alive. Upon arrival, my friend Dan and I saw a large cow moose pitifully standing on three legs gazing at the passing traffic. Further inspection revealed a bullet hole just above the knee through its right rear leg. Apparently someone in a vehicle with a rifle on board fired at the poor animal, inflicting a wound that would prove to be fatal. An animal the size of a moose cannot support its weight on three legs and therefore is doomed. Realizing its grave condition, I reluctantly decided to put it out of its misery and then try to salvage the meat. As Dan and I approached to begin the messy job of field dressing, I noticed a movement near the stomach area. I asked myself why in the world I hadn't thought of that earlier! Of course. It was carrying a calf. Maybe we could have drugged the mother or something to more protect the little one, but it was too late.

The mother being dead, I was left with no choice. I had to perform my first Caesarian on a moose.

With Dan's encouragement, I slowly and delicately made the necessary incisions to separate the little creature from its dead mother's womb. There it lay with a face only a mother moose could love—the living, breathing next generation of a poached moose. Our job now was to keep it alive. I continued to massage and slowly pump its tiny lungs. For ten minutes, it appeared that we were going to be foster fathers. But suddenly the breathing became very labored and eventually stopped altogether. Again, I had no choice on the next option, mouth-to-mouth. I had yet to use my annual CPR training on a human but I sure knew the process. Five breaths, one compression. Five breaths, one compression. Believe me it's not easy getting a seal on a moose's mouth, but I did my best. I could see the lungs expanding and there appeared to be slight signs of life. But after another five minutes, my efforts proved to be futile. Any signs of breathing had ceased and the little stressed heart just gave out. It was disappointing to sit there and reflect on the effect one joy-riding idiot had on these magnificent animals. This was the epitome of reckless disregard for a vulnerable resource. Just like many cases of this type, there was no apprehension of any suspect.

Author performing CPR on a calf moose after its mother had been illegally shot by a poacher in April.

THIRTY
The Roundabout Approaches

While making my daily rounds, I would typically concentrate my energy on fishing enforcement. With hundreds of lakes in my patrol area, occasionally I'd throw a dart at a map to point me in an arbitrary direction. I would employ this option more often on days when I had few complaint calls and nothing was considered urgent that morning. This type of general patrolling not only cleared my head but many times resulted in interesting and valuable contacts. What this little process really accomplished was to encourage me to visit areas I would normally have put on the back burner; it helped break the routine trap that can easily befall an officer. I would often think, "What a job! A $20,000 truck and all its attached goodies, a boat and motor to use at my discretion, clean (furnished) attire, and 800 square miles of water, woods and wildlife that I can visit at my whim. Oh, I forgot. I'm paid for this, too!"

My favorite modus operandi was to approach a body of water, always making an effort to remain undetected. It just made sense to me as a patrolling resource officer to take a few precautions upon arrival, even if it only resulted in a few minutes of undercover scanning. Using binoculars or the more powerful spotting scope, I could inventory sportsmen's activities prior to making the first personal exchange.

The most common indiscretion I spotted was using too many lines to take fish—more than one in the summer or more than two in the winter. Not the most flagrant of fishing violations but one that has been installed primarily to increase the number of recreational hours needed to catch a limit of fish. It's just one of the many restrictions utilized to keep the "sport" in the sport of fishing. Those that make a conscious decision to ignore this rule are certainly people with whom a warden would at least like to make an initial contact . . . sometimes one thing leads to another.

As I headed for one of my randomly selected lakes, it was a fairly cold day for March, in the high teens, but calm and rather decent conditions to enjoy some of the last and most productive crappie fishing of the winter season. During this slower activity period, I concentrated my efforts pretty much on panfishing.

Game fish season had been closed for a month, but there were always the dyed-in-the-wool fishermen who would fish right up to ice-out. I knew well the dozen or so lakes in the area that produced nice fish, and these comprised the sites I patrolled, particularly just before and after sunset.

As I slowly drove along the wooded edge of a small lake southwest of Cohasset, I spotted what appeared to be a fisherman about a half mile out in the lake's center. The heat distortion through the lens of my spotting scope blurred the view just enough so that it was impossible to detect anything suspicious. My civilian partner Dennis and I sat discussing strategy, and we both pretty much ruled out a check on this lone fishermen. There were lakes down the line that would most likely have more fishing activity.

"Hold on a second, I might have something here," I announced, as I took a last glance through the 60-power lens. "He's moving around a lot. He seems to be paying special attention to more than two holes. I think it's worth a jaunt out there. Now comes the big question. Just walking up on this guy will do little in the way of detecting a violation, especially if he is using extra lines. What do you think, Dennis? Willing to go the whole route on this one?"

"Sure. What do you have in mind?"

"Disguise. We have to look like just another couple of ice fishermen, totally indifferent to his existence. I'd guess this whole excursion will take us almost to dark. We've got about a half hour."

"Let's go for it," replied Dennis. "You lead the way."

I was aware this was a low percentage gamble at best, but I so enjoyed the challenge it was all I could do to contain my eagerness. For all I knew, he could be the straightest arrow on the planet. However, if he was using too many lines or possessed a game fish, our chances of calling his bluff would rely solely on technique and patience.

"I think we have enough gear in the truck to give the impression that we're just another couple of fishermen. Why don't you grab that bucket and stick a few fresh-cut branches in it so they protrude out the top," I motioned to Dennis. "I'll carry the old hand auger and another bucket."

The angler spotted us immediately as we eased our way through a fluffy heap onto the snow-drifted surface of the frozen lake. "Keep a slow pace at a 45-degree angle, head down," I advised Dennis. "Don't even look his direction." My plan was to get within 200 yards, drill some holes and set up as if we were fishing. I hoped at that distance our counterfeit jig sticks would look real so he would begin to get comfortable with our presence, eventually forgetting about us . . . then I could utilize the binoculars.

"This is going to take a while," I mused. "He won't stop looking our way." I felt if I even raised the glasses, he might spot the reflection or my gawking profile, and that would be the end of that! I thought, "This might be one of the more laughable ploys I've attempted." I could see myself trying to explain to the fisherman why we were hauling willow branches in a bucket and why we didn't just walk out and check him. I always had a hard time admitting to someone that I considered them a suspect for a time, especially when they were perfectly legal.

It took almost 20 minutes for our subject to lower his suspicion and focus more on his fishing than on us. This was my first hint that something might be askew—too much interest in his neighbors.

I finally stole a look in that direction. Sitting on my little bucket—we had yet to catch a thing—I could barely distinguish what appeared to be at least six mounds of snow, most likely locations of drilled holes. As I continued to sneak peeks, It appeared he was tending a line at each site. "Now's our time, Dennis. Wait until his back is to us so we close as much distance as possible before he spots us advancing." I obviously didn't possess a wealth of experience on this tactic, and it sure isn't found in your local library, but Dennis seemed impressed.

"I'm right behind ya, Tom," he mumbled, as he grabbed his undercover bucket.

To my amazement, the little scheme worked. We were only 50 feet from the guy before he picked up our stumbling motion. By this time it was not possible to get a word out. "Hold on . . . a . . . second . . . sir. Just catch . . . ing my breath! OK. That's better. How's fishin?"

"Tom, it's you. I'll be darn. Wondering who that was out there. Actually not too good." He knew it was all over.

There I was, standing among six lines, all baited and in the water. "Looks like you're a little over on lines," I pronounced.

"Yup, you got me. Good job!"

What? A compliment from a violator? It felt good . . . now Dennis was really impressed!

Same lake . . . only summer this time.

Cruising up to my trusty hiding position, I scanned the blue surface from behind the trees and spotted a boat next to shore on the opposite side of the lake. It was a real stretch for my spotting scope, but I attached it to my window and took a glimpse. It took less than a minute to observe the single fisherman working two lines. I was surprised how clear the image appeared at a half a mile, but very little of the heat that sometimes causes distortion was rising from the surface this early evening. For more than an hour, I stared through the optic until my eyes started to sting, all the time watching the boater casting and catching fish with two rods. "Won't be long now," I thought. "Getting toward sunset. He should be coming in shortly."

I parked so I would be out of sight when he returned to his car—at least that's what I thought. Apparently I failed to back up far enough, as he noticed and most likely recognized the hood of my enforcement truck protruding just beyond a clump of bushes.

I could tell right away that he spotted me because he made an immediate 90-degree turn in the middle of the lake and proceeded around a point of land where I lost sight of him. About a minute later the boat returned and pushed in through the wild rice channel to a waiting car and trailer. "How ya doing today? Any luck out there?"

"Got a few. Good lake for crappies. You know that, Tom."

"Got a job to do, though. Noticed you fishing with an extra line and have to give you a ticket." I knew this man as a decent person and extraordinarily good fisherman, so I took for granted he'd admit to the facts and accept the consequences. Wrong on that theory! He came unglued in a big way.

"What do you mean you saw me with two rods! Just take a look in the boat. What do you see? One rod, that's right, one rod! Better get your eyes examined!!"

It was always difficult for me to meet good people I knew pretty well, who had lost their sense of balance like this. He knew exactly what I saw but was instantly overpowered by that "internal defense mechanism—denial," as well as a slight bit of arrogance—-the "Not me. Do you know who you're talking to?" type of posture. He railed, "You issue me that ticket and I'm not going to sign it. You're not going to hear the end of this. I'm passing this whole thing on to my daughter. She's a lawyer, you know."

"You'll be hearing from her on Monday!" This barrage continued well after the summons was presented to him. Indeed he refused to sign it and threw the paper on the ground.

"Listen. I know you're upset and you think you beat the system by throwing your rod overboard. Your argument here isn't going to work. You'll calm down by tomorrow. Have a good day." This is one of the downsides in this occupation: being beat on by someone you thought you knew pretty well . . . for just doing your job. It's one of those things you learn to take in stride.

The following morning helped boost my faith in humanity. My fisherman buddy called me at 8:00 a.m., somewhat apologizing for his irate behavior. "I've thought about it, Tom, and I'm just going to pay the ticket . . . not worth the hassle." (Notice the lack of admission, however.)

My response was, "Good decision. I figured you'd come around. You're a good man." And he really was. The pressure of the moment was just too much to deal with; he needed a longer cooling-off period than most. Should such a person be classified as a poacher? Technically, yes. Even a small violation like two-lining can assign you to this status. But in my mind a real "poacher" is one who, despite the penalties applied, fails to get the message. He got the message.

One more . . . same lake!

The snow had all melted about a week before on this spring day in early April. But there was still 2 feet of ice on the lakes, so fishermen were continuing to angle for panfish, even though the walleye and northern pike season had been closed for more than six weeks.

At 40 degrees, the sun had reduced the lake's surface to a glossy, smooth-looking, water-like image and made it so slick that it was even difficult to stand up, let alone walk.

As I surveyed the little lake from my open truck window, there appeared to be a group of human figures out in the middle. My binoculars soon confirmed that four people were fishing. The wavy heat rays rising from the warming surface made it impossible to distinguish any fish on the ice, but the group's location raised my curiosity; it was more of a northern pike haunt than a panfish location. I thought to myself, "It's going to be the challenge of the day to check these guys, especially if they have illegal fish in possession."

I unloaded my snowmobile out of the truck box and deliberated on a plan. "I could try the old time-tested angle approach again, but that would be a long shot. The minute they hear the engine and see the machine on the ice, a couple of kicks, and back into the holes go the fish. What the heck," I thought, "let's take a crack at it."

Again, I would have to convince them that I wasn't a threat. Not a small task with a state-issued snowmobile suit and snowmobile. I slowly motored up along the shoreline to get within range of my field glasses. I was halfway there. Now I could sneak a quick look at their setup. I walked into the alder brush for cover and watched. They appeared aware of my movements but weren't as concerned as I would have thought . . . considering they had at least four illegal fish lying on the ice!

I continued to play around in the brush for a while trying to give the impression that my attention was on something else other than them. Following a short walk along the brushy bank, I jumped on my snowmobile and angled their way. I had 300 yards to cover before they figured me out and deep-sixed the evidence. The ice was so extremely slippery that I had to start out very slowly just to acquire traction. It took a half minute to get up any speed and then at 30 miles per hour, I realized it was impossible to steer, let alone stop. If I slowed down at all, my element of semi-surprise would be lost. My only chance for quick justice was to let the machine continue its course and jump off as it was slowing down, hopefully foot-sliding into the bunch.

As my weight left the machine, I managed to stay upright during my first 20 feet of uncontrolled glide, while the snowmobile continued its driverless trip down the lake. However, I overestimated my speed's rate of decrease; I experienced zero resistance on the polished ice. My hands were now straight out, knees bent and body hunched, pretty much resembling a ski jumper ready to launch. I noticed the men gawking as I slid over their holes and around their buckets, finally tripping on an ice chunk and landing facedown on two of the after-season pike. Clinging to my last shred of professionalism, I shot up to a standing position and announced, "Game warden. Arrived to check your fish!"

"I knew that was him . . . I knew that was him," I overheard one of the parties mumbling. "That's quite an approach you just made. You always do that?"

"Only when its necessary, and I can see that's the case here," as I pointed to the spread of five illegal fish below me. What I didn't describe was the terror of being out of control for those few seconds.

Further particulars of the arrests aren't necessary to reveal other than another comment I overheard: "I told you guys we should have kicked those back in the hole."